GW00871222

'In praise of ladies dead and lovely knights'

Shakespeare, Sonnet 106

Rubbings can be taken from manhole covers, pillar boxes, gravestones and of course church brasses. This book contains everything you need to know about this increasingly popular activity: locations, methods, different techniques for achieving original results, and the many varied uses to which the finished product can be put, for simple wall hangings to decorative place mats. Unique features are an easy-reference section covering the top thirty church brasses in Britain and a complete list of dated brasses in all London churches.

Widen Your Horizons with this series

Remember that we cater for all interests. See for yourself with our varied list of titles.

Places to see

Scottish Islands – Tom Weir
Dartmoor – Crispin Gill

Leisure activities

Good Photography Made Easy – Derek Watkins
Cine Photography Made Easy – Derek Watkins
Looking at Churches – David Bowen
Railways for Pleasure –Geoffrey Body
The Antique-Hunter's Handbook – Ronald Rawlings
Wine and Beer Making – Derek Watkins

Sporting

The Art of Good Shooting – J. E. M. Ruffer
Archery for All – Daniel Roberts
Rowing for Everyone – Christopher Chant
Sea Fishing for Fun – Alan Wrangles and Jack P. Tupper

Holidays

Pony Trekking –Edward Hart
Inland Waterways – Charles Hadfield

Brass and Other Rubbings

Emma Wood

David & Charles
Newton Abbot London
North Pomfret (Vt) Vancouver

Cover: Top row from left to right – Thailand stone rubbing; brass rubbing of Elizabeth Culpeper, d. 1634, aged 7; Margaret Peyton, d. 1484; Bottom – 'dog with its head in a pot' coal plate rubbing

British Library Cataloguing in Publication Data

Wood, Emma
Brass and other rubbings. – (David & Charles leisure and travel series).
1. Rubbings
I. Title II. Series
760 NC915.R8

ISBN 0-7153-7500-8

Library of Congress Catalog Card Number 77-91731

Photographs by the author except where stated

Typeset by Tradespools Limited, Frome
and printed in Great Britain by
Redwood Burn Limited, Trowbridge & Esher
for David & Charles (Publishers) Limited
Brunel House Newton Abbot Devon

Published in the United States of America
by David & Charles Inc
North Pomfret Vermont 05053 USA

Published in Canada
by Douglas David & Charles Limited
1875 Welch Street North Vancouver BC

Contents

Turn Left
BRASS
RUBBING
in
St Margaret's
Church
Open Daily Except Sundays

Introduction

Making rubbings is fun. Whatever the subject – monumental brasses, gravestones, coal-hole covers, a pattern of leaves or any textured surface – the activity is in itself enjoyable and the end result pleasing. Rubbing can also be educational, leading to a widening historical awareness and experimentation with craft techniques.

Let us be clear then from the outset that this is a book about *rubbings*, how to take them using different methods and materials, and the many and varied uses to which they can be put. Much incidental information is given too on the types of objects which can be rubbed, especially brasses, and I hope that readers will be interested enough to find out more about these fascinating topics from the many excellent specialist publications available, some of which are noted in the bibliography.

I think it important to make the distinction early on between so-called academic and popular attitudes to rubbing, of brasses in particular. All too often 'decorative' rubbers, as opposed to archivists, are denigrated for their apparent lack of in-depth involvement. Indeed, one eminent author on brasses states firmly that he disapproves of brass rubbing for fun, condemning those who do it as being 'wallpaper minded' and, whilst not going so far as to accuse them of violating sacred ground, does consider entering churches for the purpose of producing attractive wall-hangings as some kind of 'spiritual trespass'.

The current expansion of brass rubbing centres, most of which are on ecclesiastical property, usually in the churches themselves, and run with the full blessing of the clergy, gives the lie to this. So too does my own introduction to brass rubbing by a Reverend Professor whose fine regency dining room was surrounded from low cornice to ceiling with magnificent six-foot high figures of knights, ladies and priests who looked down on the 'feasting' below with a fastidious and seemingly benevolent gaze. The Professor, an authority on brasses, had made all the rubbings himself and was fully aware of their artistic effect. He considered that, even for an unbeliever, there were far worse activities than being on one's knees in a place of worship, indulging in fairly strenuous effort, imbibing the peaceful atmosphere and the beauty of the brass and its surroundings. He pointed out, with a twinkle in his eye, that his own dog-collar obviously facilitated relationships with fellow clergymen who might otherwise be suspicious – and perhaps rightly so – of people turning up out of the blue to wear away just a fraction more from some priceless medieval monument.

Admittedly that was some fifteen years ago, before the real rubbing boom of the early 'seventies when more and more people, especially visitors to Britain, took it up as an increasingly popular spare-time activity. I was lucky in that when I started rubbing most parish priests were delighted to find intelligent interest being taken in their treasures. Having the courtesy to make a prior appointment, acting responsibly 'on site' and contributing a little something to the building maintenance fund at the end of the day, meant that most churches were open to the enthusiast who took the trouble to make often long journeys to sometimes isolated villages in search of good examples of particular styles or periods.

The same conditions do still prevail today in the more out of the way places where visitors are few and brasses not especially noteworthy, and I would be the first to encourage keen students of the craft of rubbing to be prepared to make a detour or a special foray to a place which is known to have monuments. But in many of the more accessible spots – churches in and within easy distance of London, Oxford, Cambridge and the prime tourist areas – well-meaning brass rubbers have become a real menace, involving the incumbents in a complicated system of appointments and payments and, more important, constituting a genuine threat to the fabric as they 'scrub away' at the brasses and leave their own impressions, however slight, on the surrounding stone.

As a result several churches no longer permit rubbing and in some cases the brasses are protected behind glass or moved from their original position on the floor to an inaccessible one high on the walls. This has led to the establishment of several countrywide specialist 'rubbing centres' (see Appendix C) where some seventy or so facsimile brasses are available for beginners or the keen amateur. Exact replicas of the originals, these brasses are made by craftsmen with the full cooperation of the churches involved and the centres are, in the main, run by experienced, well-meaning people con-

2 Rubbing a facsimile of the fine military brass to Sir Robert de Bures (1331) at the London Brass Rubbing Centre. A finished rubbing hangs above (*British Tourist Authority*)

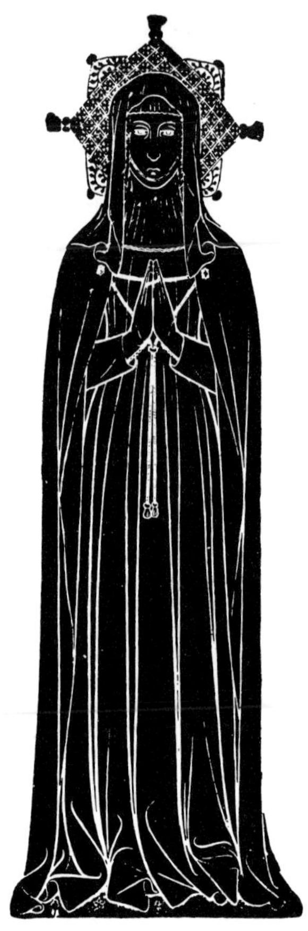

3 Medieval brass to the Duchess of Gloucester, Alianore de Bohun (1399) in Westminster Abbey

cerned to preserve the old brasses whilst making the information they hold more available for use in schools and craft classes.

At first I must confess to having been rather wary of such places which seemed to smack of commercial exploitation and, given a choice, would obviously prefer a solitary hour or so in a quiet church with an unusual brass and the opportunity to concentrate on my own thoughts as well as the rubbing. And indeed anyone hoping to take away anything more meaningful than an actual rubbing would do well not to venture into, say Westminster Abbey in the height of summer, where at any given time some fifty or so can be counted cheek by jowl producing replicas of the facsimiles available in St Margaret's. How much more they might gain in visiting the Abbey itself and simply studying the magnificent 1399 brass of Alianore de Bohun, Duchess of Gloucester (illustration 3).

Yet I would recommend the beginner, and particularly those with children, to try their hand first at one of these centres before venturing into a church. In fact, some churches now demand proof of previous experience before they permit rubbing, so trial runs using different techniques and materials do not come amiss. Also, the timid may take advantage of the instruction which is usually provided or take comfort from the efforts of their fellow rubbers, whilst the gregarious can strike up conversations with neighbours from all over the country, from Europe, Australia, Canada, the USA and the Far East.

Wherever the brass rubber works he or she will absorb, whether consciously or not, details of the figures, whether it be ladies' dress, armour or ecclesiastical vestments, children or animals, or simply different types of inscriptions. All these can be further studied and collections built up, devoted perhaps to a particular period, to knights or civilians. In the same way individual preferences can be reflected in collections of all sorts of rubbings – wall plaques, gravestones and other intriguing indented surfaces – which will be covered in the following pages.

I have enjoyed preparing this book. Research has taken me from jam-packed London rubbing centres to sleepy Dorset churchyards. I have chatted with curious children while squatting on city pavements rubbing coal-hole covers, made the acquaintance of passing policemen while balancing precariously on a make-shift ladder to record the site of a famous theatre, and made friends with suppliers of fine papers, cork and other sundries. My store of rubbings has increased and so, I trust, has my fund of knowledge. I hope that readers will experience the same pleasure and perhaps learn something new too. And, if final proof of the joy of making one's own rubbings is needed, the words of American Lorilee Thomas, describing her last year's visit to the brass rubbing centre at St James's Church, Piccadilly, say it all. Her entry in the Visitor's Book sums up the feelings of scores of other enthusiasts when she pronounces it to have been 'the height of my London visit'. Enjoy your rubbing!

1 What to Rub – Memorial Stones

Monumental Brasses

Having said very positively that this is, in the main, a book about rubbings, I must stress equally the importance of distinguishing between a rubbing and the object from which it is made. That may seem an unnecessary distinction, but it is remarkable how many people can be overheard in churches seeking brass *rubbings* rather than brasses pure and simple. Nothing is more annoying to the student of brasses, nor gives more ammunition to the anti-rubbing brigade, so for heaven's sake do have enough respect for what you are doing to absorb a little basic information.

A monumental brass is first of all a memorial which usually fulfils a practical function by covering a grave. It consists of a flat brass plate engraved with inscriptions, figures of the dead, shields of arms and other items, set in stone. Introduced in the late thirteenth century, memorial brasses were most fashionable during the next two hundred years, and though brasses are still made the vogue had really ended by the close of the sixteenth century. Yet, despite the ravages of time, including Reformation fervour, civil strife and wars – the brasses of Coventry Cathedral, for example, being destroyed as late as World War II – some 8,000 brasses survive today. In some cases the figure is estimated to be 10,000 including inscriptions, of which 4,000 are figure brasses.

The greatest concentration of these is to be found around London, in the home counties of Kent and Essex and the eastern counties of Suffolk and Norfolk, some of the wealthiest areas of the country in the Middle Ages and also those with no local stone for monuments. Other counties such as Lincolnshire and Gloucestershire with a large number of well-off merchants, particularly in the wool trade, are also well represented, but the northern parts have few brasses. Scotland possesses only six and there are five in Ireland.

Brasses are not restricted to the British Isles however, and indeed the earliest-known existing brass is in Germany, whilst there are many other notable examples in north-west and central Europe, especially Belgium, Holland and Poland. Some sixteen or so continental brasses can be found in England, all in the intricate 'Flemish' style, with detailed backgrounds as opposed to the clean, uncluttered lines of early English brasses. Excellent examples of these large, decorated, tapestry-like brasses are to be found at King's Lynn, Norfolk (Adam de Walsokne, d. 1349 and his wife), St Albans Abbey, Herts (Abbot Thomas de la Mare, d. c 1370–80) and a later one at All Hallows, by the Tower of London (A. Evyngar, d. 1533 and wife).

By contrast, contemporary English brasses are exceedingly plain, simple recumbent figures in an attitude of prayer, with heads frequently supported by pillows and feet on small animals. Canopies were sometimes introduced, as on sculptured stone monuments, but apart from the inscription and the occasional heraldic device there were no other trimmings. All the deceased look alike, stylized figures devoid of personality, furrows or warts, representing calm, solid virtue. Such simplistic design declined in the late 1300s and had virtually ceased by the beginning of the sixteenth century when Renaissance influences brought about a revival in the art with more individual portraits and figures in 'active' positions, kneeling, holding hands (illustration 5) and even a hunter shooting a deer while Death, in the form of a skeleton stabs them both (James Gray, d. 1591, Hunsdon, Herts).

Changes in style were allied to variations in subject matter. Early brasses are devoted to knights – local landowners rather than military men – their wives and wealthy merchants. By the fifteenth century small traders began to appear on brasses, with memorials to bakers, blacksmiths and brewers. There is even a pair of gloves to commemorate Peter Denot, a glover who died c 1440 at Fletching, Sussex. And by the sixteenth century the majority of the middle classes were able to afford a brass, complete with stone for around £2, which it is estimated would cost well over £100 today.

Here then in a single art form is a vast panoply of English life from medieval times to the present. Here are the knights, squires, burgers and their respective wives and families, priests, lawyers and academics who represent the respectable social classes over some 800 years. Through their portraits can be traced the outlines of English history, recorded in changes of *dramatis personae* – from aristocracy to fishmonger – fashions in costume, covering armour, women's dress, ecclesiastical vestments and civilian garments, and the development of language from Norman French, through Latin to English.

Men in Armour

The oldest brass in the country is that of Sir John d'Aubernoun, d. 1277, at Stoke d'Abernon, Surrey (illustration 4). A noble figure standing six-foot high (early brasses were usually life size) he is clad entirely in mail – thousands of interlinked iron rings – the same kind of armour as that worn by the English forces at the Battle of Hastings in 1066. This was composed of a hood with a metal or leather skull cap inside (*coif-de-mailles*), a sleeved shirt which covered the hands as gloves (*hauberk*) and stockings to the toes (*chausses*). His knees are reinforced with leather caps (*poleyns*) and he has pointed prick spurs. Over the mail he wears a surcoat, a simple cloth garment cut away below the waist in front to facilitate movement, and drawn in at the middle by a cord.

Sir John is unusual in that he is the only known example of a major figure on a brass who carries a lance. His shield – *azure, a chevron or* – is also rare in that it still bears much of the original blue enamel. Colouring was frequently used to denote armorial bearings on later brasses, though little remains today. The delicate enamel is a real hazard for unwary rubbers as it must *not* be rubbed. Simply trace the outline of the shield and fill it in later. I made what now seems an obvious error of colouring the arms, which looks most unreal as the blue and gold stands out from the black rubbing instead of blending with the bronze tones of the actual brass. Far better to stick to a complementary black and white shield, filling in the dense black at home with the same type of wax.

No facsimile of this brass exists so those wishing to make a rubbing must visit the little village of Stoke d'Abernon near Kingston-on-Thames. As usual, an appointment should be made and a small fee is charged, but any inconvenience is far outweighed by the magnificent brass which makes a most impressive rubbing. Obviously every rubbing of a brass of this age is detrimental and the enamel is especially prone to damage, so do act responsibly if you are lucky enough to rub it.

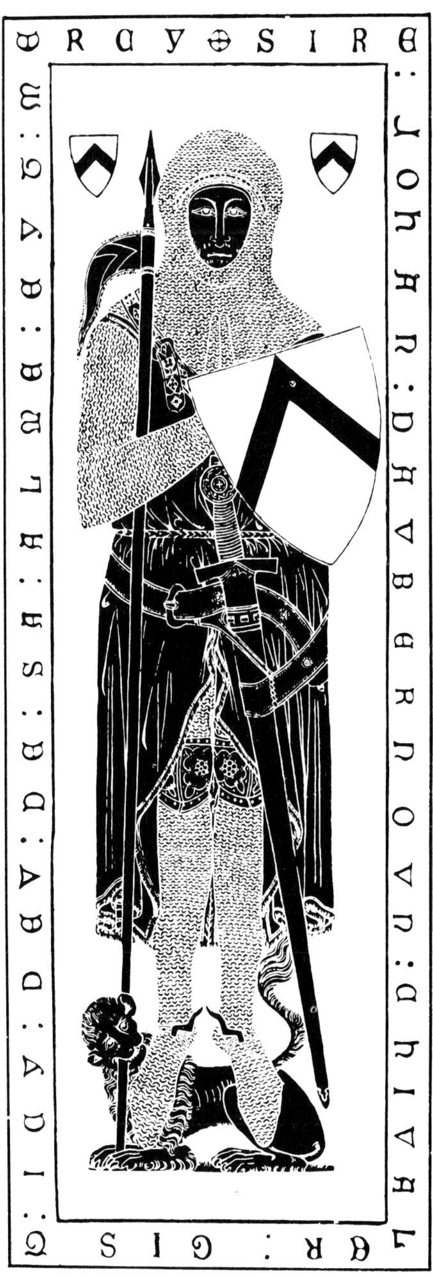

4 The oldest British brass to Sir John d'Aubernoun (1277) at Stoke d'Abernon, Surrey, is an excellent example of complete mail armour

Fortunately a similar brass of the complete mail period has been produced in facsimile and is available at several rubbing centres (illustration 2). Described as 'the finest military brass in existence' it commemorates Sir Robert de Bures, d. 1331, from Acton, near Long Melford in Suffolk. Like the brass to Sir John d'Aubernoun, the original is unusual among the few remaining early military brasses in that it was entirely completed before being put down.

Both goldsmiths and stonemasons have been recognized as working on important brasses, though until the end of the sixteenth century specific workshops produced both the brass and its setting so that the brass engraver had to be able to work in stone also. The brass sheets were made of latten, an alloy of copper and zinc with a little lead, quite unlike modern brass in composition and appearance. The plates were quite small, the largest being about 3 ft square, and consequently had to be joined for the larger brasses. After the design had been approved, it was traced on the metal then engraved with a v-shaped burin, a tool still used today. Cut from the plate and frequently coloured, the figure was then riveted to the stone – often of Purbeck marble – which had previously been chiselled out to the exact shape and depth of the brass so that when completed the two surfaces would lie flush.

Where thousands of brasses have been destroyed the stone matrix, or indent as it is called still remains, affording some idea of the size and wealth of those brasses, one such being the slab still in Durham Cathedral which housed the magnificent memorial to Bishop Beaumont. If making rubbings as records rather than just decoration, it is advisable to include the outline of any missing parts of the original brass as revealed by the indent, including arms, canopy and inscription. Whilst historically accurate this is not particularly attractive, so those wishing simply to make decorative wall hangings should avoid mutilated or incomplete brasses.

On outstanding brasses, however, it is sometimes possible to 'cheat' to obtain a complete figure. In the line reproduction of the brass to John Hauley and his two wives at Dartmouth, Devon (illustration 5) all three figures are shown complete. Yet, as illustration 35 of a poor-quality rubbing shows, part of one arm of the wife who stands alone on her husband's left is missing from the actual brass. When, as in this case, an exact model of the missing piece is

5 An impressive brass at St Saviour's, Dartmouth, Devon, to John Hauley and his two wives (1408). Compare the female figure standing alone with illustration 35, page 78

available in the other arm, it is but a few minutes' task to trace the outline, then reverse it before attaching it to the rest of the rubbing and filling in any necessary detail with wax.

The 1408 figure of Hauley himself – the naval town's most distinguished citizen – is a good example of the transitional period in English armour when, in an attempt to keep pace with increasingly

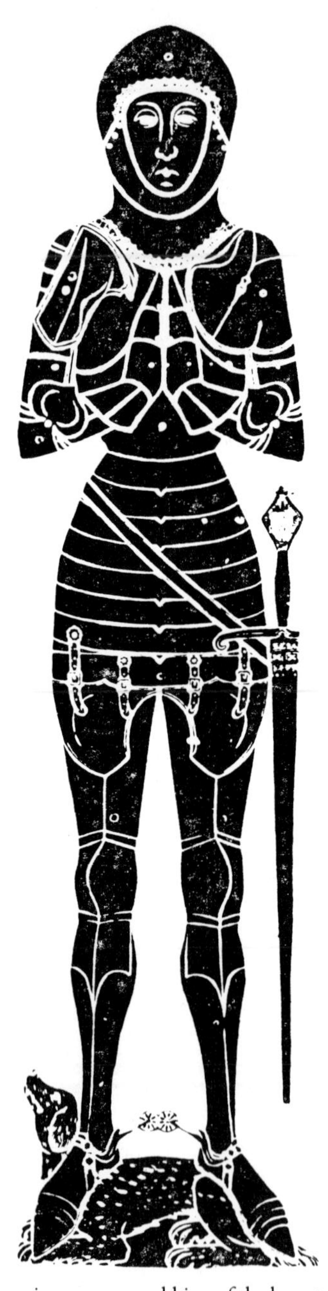

6 Showing the full plate era in armour, a rubbing of the brass to Richard Dixton (1438) from Cirencester, Glos

7 Lion at the feet of Sir John Foljambe, St John the Baptist, Tideswell, Derbyshire (for full figure see illustration 31)

lethal weapons, plate began to replace mail. Hauley's legs are protected by plate greaves with pointed plate sabatons on his feet. His arms are similarly covered and he wears a pointed steel helmet, the bascinet, from which hangs the camail to protect the neck and throat. By this time the surcoat had been replaced by the short, tight-fitting jupon, with a rigid baldric worn around the hips taking over from the old loose sword-belt.

Until 1410 all military brasses were depicted in similar armour to this, presenting a virtually uniform appearance for half a century or so. The full plate era which followed is well represented on brasses, a good late example being that of Richard Dixton, d. 1438, in Cirencester, Glos, which is available in facsimile for rubbing (illustration 6). Later developments were all designed to make armour less unwieldy, one noteworthy event towards the end of the fifteenth century being the sudden change to round-toed shoes from the extreme pointed Gothic style. This was caused by a 1463 Act of Parliament forbidding footwear, civilian as well as military, with points more than two inches long!

Much of the pleasure in recognizing and dating armour lies in acquiring enough knowledge to be able to discount the unsubstantiated stories which many people still accept as fact. For instance, it was long believed that if a knight on a brass had his feet resting on a lion, as with Sir John d'Aubernoun, he had died in battle, whereas a knight such as Richard Dixton with his feet on a dog or other animal had died in peacetime. In fact, lions simply signify courage – and indeed some ladies on brasses also have lions at their feet – and the dog stands for sporting interests when not a specific family pet.

Similarly, military figures in a cross-legged pose were said to have been Crusaders, although the Crusades were more or less finished when brasses became fashionable and only Sir Roger de Trumpington, d. 1289, whose brass can be seen in the village church at Trumpington, near Cambridge, is known to have taken the Cross with Prince Edward in 1270. The crossed legs on most brasses were probably only to meet the architectural taste of the times which favoured 'movement' as opposed to straight lines.

Ladies

If most of us automatically think of brasses as huge knights in armour more and more people prefer to make rubbings of the delicate, often exquisitely dressed ladies who accompany their husbands on brasses. The earliest civilian brasses are to women, the first being that of Margaret, Lady Camoys, d. 1310, at Trotton, near Midhurst, Sussex, which is a little unusual in that she was unmarried. (The later, previously mentioned Westminster Abbey brass to Alianore de Bohun, page 10, who was a widow, depicts her as a 'vowess'.)

Early brasses show females attired in kirtles, loose long gowns, with a kerchief over the head and a wimple covering the chin. The kirtle was replaced after 1350 by the *côte-hardie*, a close-fitting top with sleeves to the elbow and long lappets falling to the ground, and a flowing skirt. A cloak or mantle was often draped over the shoulders and fastened across the front. The two wives of John Hauley (page 17) are wearing the peculiar garment known as the sideless *côte-hardie*, the outer dress being cut away at the sides to reveal a tight under-dress, which was immensely popular from 1370.

Perhaps the part of female apparel which has most captured the

8 Butterfly head-dress as seen on the brass to Margaret Peyton (1484)

imagination is the head-dress, which went through many and varied changes throughout the fifteenth century and is amply illustrated on brasses of the time. When the simple kerchief was abandoned, hair was first plaited, laced with ribbons and gathered on either side of the face as worn by John Hauley's wives. Gradually these 'bosses' of hair were drawn back from the head, extended upwards and outwards and covered with an embroidered kerchief to form the horned head-dress.

From 1470 the head-dress achieved its most elegant form, the butterfly style where the hair was swept back and secured in a lace net, surrounded by a transparent veil supported on a wire frame and falling down behind to give the impression of butterflies' wings. One of the most well-known brasses showing this lovely style is that of Margaret Peyton, c. 1484 (cover and illustration 8). The first wife of Thomas Peyton of Isleham, Cambridge, she stands on his right hand with the second wife, another Margaret, in a similar head-dress on the left. All three figures have been produced in facsimile and the 'first' Margaret, known as 'the Lace lady' from the beautiful design on her dress, is deservedly popular with rubbing enthusiasts. Her waisted, *décolleté* gown with turned-down collar and cuffs, is in a rich brocade or cut velvet. She wears an elaborate necklace and her head is turned sideways to show off the fine butterfly head-dress which carries the words 'Lady Jhu Mercy'.

This extremely feminine head-dress was replaced at the end of the fifteenth century by the unflattering gabled head-dress with its long 'ears' which were eventually shortened to form the severe French hood in the second half of Henry VIII's reign. Hats, puffed sleeves and hooped skirts were worn by Tudor ladies, and while there are some attractive Elizabethan brasses of women wearing ruffs, slashed-sleeve bodices and embroidered petticoats, later examples of female dress can best be seen from contemporary illustrations and are not really the concern of brasses.

Men and Clergy

While women's fashions went through as many shifts as they do today – shifts which were fully charted on brasses – changes in men's dress were not recorded in any detail as most civilians of the Middle Ages wore long gowns which covered up all under-garments. The

9 Head of a wool merchant from a c 1400 brass at Northleach, Glos

way in which hair was worn is perhaps the most accurate dating device, fourteenth-century full beards being replaced by two small tufts on the chin in the early 1400s, as shown in a brass of this time to a wool merchant from Northleach, Glos (illustration 9).

After 1420 most men were depicted as being clean-shaven with 'pudding basin' hair styles, until the reappearance of the beard in the reign of Henry VIII. Only the clergy, both secular and monastic, were allowed some variation in dress and stance up to this time, the number of vestments shown on brasses increasing with the rank held. Most ecclesiastical brasses are to parish priests, from lower ranked orders, bareheaded with a tonsure, wearing a simple cassock, through those dressed in alb and chasuble, to the full processional cope. Some priests carry chalices and the seven bishops on brasses all hold the crozier. There are brasses to three archbishops to be found in York Minster, New College, Oxford and Chigwell, Essex. Few monastic brasses survived the Reformation.

The fifteenth century vogue for melancholy *memento mori* resulted in grisly brasses of skeletons and shrouded cadavers – one even shown being eaten by worms; the wearing of arms on dress, with merchants displaying the marks of their guild or trade; the architectural detail reflected on brasses, from perpendicular canopies to designs with figures supported by brackets and a cross: all these fascinating topics are outside the scope of this volume, but by now it is hoped that the casual brass rubber will have gained some new insights and have begun to see the possibilities for further examination of allied subjects.

Those with little historical leaning may gain more pleasure from searching out unusual inscriptions which record all kinds of triumphs and disasters. Many brasses praise the dead for their generosity in life, some rail against departing this earth while others accept death with fortitude. There are several sentimental epitaphs but few attempts at humour. One of my own favourite inscriptions is on the brass to John and Ellyne Orgone, 1584, in St Olave's Church, Hart Street in the City of London. This reads:

> As I was, so be ye; as I am, you shall be,
> What I gave, that I have; what I spent, that I had:
> Thus I count all my Cost; what I left, that I lost.

The brass is in no other way outstanding, comprising two small figures in sixteenth-century dress, although the representation of the wool pack with a trade mark on it is of interest. Incidentally, St Olave's, Samuel Pepys 'own church', contains monuments to the famous diarist and his wife, and is well worth a visit.

Children

A typically tragic event of the times, death in child-birth, is catalogued by the inscription accompanying the brass to Anne Awode, d. 1512, at Blickling, Norfolk, who '. . .was brought to bed of male and female and after a perilous bearing suddenly migrated to the most blessed Lord Christ . . .'. Anne is portrayed (illustration 10) with her two dead infants in her arms. Wrapped in swaddling clothes, they are termed chrysoms, children who died within a month of birth or baptism, from the practice of placing a white cloth annointed with 'chrysm', consecrated oil, over the face at baptism.

Children on brasses make another unusual study. Families are frequently portrayed together, the children being somewhat smaller figures than their parents. Many remaining brasses date from the fifteenth century when the fashion was to group offspring below their parents, father with sons and mother with daughters. Single girls were shown with hair hanging loose, while married daughters wore caps.

Individual brasses to young children are comparatively rare so keen brass rubbers are delighted to find the charming facsimile available at many centres of little Elizabeth Culpeper, d. 1634, aged

10 Brass to Anne Awode, Blickling, Norfolk (1512) who died in child-birth, with her two dead infants

only seven (see cover). Dressed like her grandmother of the same name, who had died the previous year, young Elizabeth probably only featured as a brass because an engraver was already employed at the time preparing the old woman's memorial. It is thought certain that the same hand produced both.

Gravestones

Making rubbings from gravestones seems to have limited appeal in comparison with rubbing brasses. It is easy to see why. First, few tombstones have historically accurate images of the dead depicted on them. Then, churchyard headstones, having been subject to the elements over centuries are frequently worn away, so that rubbing them produces a poor result; it can also be harmful to the stone. Equally important to fair-weather rubbers, working on gravestones often involves exposing oneself to those same elements. Also, the usually upright stones are in themselves difficult to rub with their multi-faceted surfaces as opposed to the incised lines on flat plates of brasses, so that the impression is not always as attractive as the design. Finally, many people are quite happy to spend time in a church or at a sociable rubbing centre but find a few hours in an actual graveyard disturbing.

This is obviously a matter of personal choice. I always find churchyards immensely reassuring places, their peacefulness and timeless nature being particularly appealing. The sites of ancient pagan ceremonies, many churchyards are older than the buildings which they house and can certainly be thought of as places of joyous worship rather than mouldering burial grounds. Medieval feast days would see games and dancing in the churchyard, rather like in church halls today. Fairs would be held in 'God's acre' as the ground round the church was called, with travelling salespeople setting up booths there.

Yet many superstitions did surround graveyards and were taken quite seriously by our ancestors. For instance, the devil was thought to hold sway over the north side of the churchyard which is why unbaptized children, vagrants and suicides were buried there. The first grave in a new plot was also thought to bode ill, so an animal rather than a human was usually given the very first burial. Equally, the last person buried in a churchyard had to be laid to rest head first so as to avoid having to keep watch over all the other graves until the end of time, as it was commonly believed that the latest member of the churchyard looked after those who had gone before and only relinquished this task when a new burial occurred. Pity the last one to be buried in the conventional position before a decision to close the graveyard had been made!

Churchyard graves are usually marked in one of two main ways, table tombs or head stones. Like the altar-tombs inside the church, table tombs usually commemorated wealthy citizens. The main advantage of this type of memorial was that, being raised above the ground, it did not become overgrown with weeds. The tops of such tombs nearest the church door were used as real tables for the distribution of bread and ale to the poor from funds provided in the wills of generous benefactors. Some churches, however, had wooden bread shelves inside the actual building which fulfilled the same purpose. Indeed, at the amazing black-and-white 'Jacobean' church of St Oswald, Lower Peover, Cheshire, a loaf is still left on the ancient bread shelves each Sunday.

Illustration 11 of the churchyard of St Andrew, Enfield, shows plain and sculptured tombs surrounded by many plain stone slabs set in the earth. Until the middle of the nineteenth century it was acceptable to exhume old remains and reuse the graves, simply laying down the previous tablet so that some churchyards are almost paved with ancient stones. It was estimated that, in the hundred years or so up to 1823, over 10,000 were buried at St Andrew's, and the present churchyard contains a number of interesting old memorials. One large tomb to a John White, a surveyor with the New River Company, records somewhat tongue-in-cheek that

> Here lies John White, who, day by day,
> On river works did use much clay,
> Is now himself turning that way.

St Andrew's also contains a very fine brass to Lady Tiptoft, d. 1446. Set on the top of a large altar tomb, the brass figure is surrounded by an heraldic canopy in good order.

Headstones fulfilled the same function as wall tablets within the church. It is rare to find one earlier than the sixteenth century. Up to

11 Part of the churchyard of St Andrew, Enfield, with tombs and gravestones laid flat

1800 most gravestones were low standing but very substantial. Many were carved with symbolic figures such as a serpent forming a circle by biting its tail, representing Eternity, and a scythe for Death the reaper. Later, wings, angels and an open book are quite common, and later still these were replaced by classic burial urns and elaborate scrolls.

Commemorative stones *inside* churches should not be discounted as such monumental slabs were, in the main, to the landed classes, and thus contain elaborate representations or interesting inscriptions. In the parish church at Presbury, Cheshire, for instance, while there are no figure brasses nor sculptured effigies of knights in armour, there are several historic tablets. One most attractive incised alabaster slab shows Jasper Worth, d. 1592, and his wife Alice. Beneath her feet stand three children and two shields of arms are also shown. The stone, like the one to Robert Downes, d. 1495, and Emma his wife, is now set into the church wall, although originally the top of an altar-tomb. Similarly, a stone to Edward Warren, d. 1558, showing him in full plate armour with his head resting on the helmet, just as on military brasses, and an elaborately engraved Calvary Cross with inscription on the border, are now fixed to the north wall of the chancel. Such unusual monuments make most attractive rubbings.

An interesting incised slab stands against a wall in the Farnham Chapel at St Bartholomew's Quorndon, Leicester. Thomas Farnham, d. 1500, wears plate armour and is shown with his wife. The crudely-drawn figures, far more life-like than contemporary brasses, are quite unlike any others in this country, bearing a close resemblance to carvings found in Italian churches.

More commonplace incised tomb slabs are still to be found in many church floors, however. The majority contain inscriptions while some show shields of arms. For those interested in this type of memorial, a good collection of stone rubbings of heraldic medallions can be found catalogued in London's Victoria and Albert Museum. Such slabs can be rubbed with wax in the same way as brasses (page 54) and make equally arresting forms of decoration.

Church interiors, in general, will have something to delight the historian and lover of the arts, as well as frequently producing some unusual memorial. Inside St Mary's, Rotherhithe, close to the

12 Interior of St Mary's, Rotherhithe, East London

London docks (illustration 12) is a tablet to Christopher Jones, master of the *Mayflower,* who died shortly after returning from that famous voyage with the Pilgrim Fathers. And, while 'the most complete ancient organ in London', made by John Byfield in 1764, may claim immediate attention, closer scrutiny of the walls will reveal a marble stone which reads:

> In the adjacent churchyard lies the body of
> Prince Lee Boo,
> Son of Abba Thulle, Rupack or King of the Island
> Cooroora, one of the Pelew or Palos Islands,

and records the death from small-pox, at the age of twenty, of this same prince, who had been brought to England by a Captain Wilson of Rotherhithe after his ship had been wrecked on Lee Boo's native island. The brick tomb is still in the churchyard though the inscription is much weathered and certainly impossible to rub.

Such tombs and headstones repay further study, for as well as recording the bald facts of who is buried there and when they died, the inscriptions are often sad, sometimes poetic, at times startling and frequently humorous. The obituary writer can be seen tying himself in knots in order to gain 'felicitous' rhymes as with this curious epitaph in the churchyard at Whitchurch, Hants:

> This grave, Oh greife, hath swallowed up, with wide and open mouth, The body of good Richard Brooke, of Whitchurch, Hampton south.

Hampshire is technically within the old county of Southampton, and the writer has transposed the two parts of the Southampton name to gain his rhyming couplet!

And how much incidental knowledge we can pick up from browsing through churchyards. The beautiful twelfth-century church of St Mary at Shrewsbury, Shropshire, well worth a visit in its own right, was the literal downfall of a steeple-jack called Cadman in 1739. After repairing the spire, he took it in mind to reach the ground by means of a rope fastened from the weathercock to a tree on the other side of the river. His epitaph records this unwise move and 'his fatal end':

Let this small monument record the name
Of Cadman and to future time proclaim
How by a bold attempt to fly from this high spire,
Across the Sabrine stream he did acquire
His fatal end. 'Twas not from want of skill
Or courage to perform the task he fell.
No, no; a faulty rope being drawn too tight
Hurried his soul on high to take its flight,
And bade the body here a last good-night.

Seekers of the famous will naturally visit the churches where their heroes are buried. Shakespeare's grave, for instance, in the chancel of Holy Trinity, Stratford, is one obvious place of pilgrimage. The words of the strangely threatening verse on the stone were set down in the dramatist's will:

Good frend for Jesus sake forbeare
To digg the dust encloased heare;
Blest be ye man yt spares thes stones,
And curst be he yt moves my bones.

As its churches are rich in brasses, so London's graveyards hold stones to many eminent persons. The ancient burial ground of Bunhill Fields, City Road, EC2 (illustrations 13 and 14) was certainly used for this purpose before 1549 when bones from the charnel-house of nearby St Paul's Cathedral were moved there. A new churchyard, planned to take plague victims was established, and was later much used by Nonconformists, being the one place where they could bury their dead without the presence of an Anglican minister. There are tombs to such notables as *Pilgrim's Progress* author, John Bunyan, Isaac Watts, 'the father of the English hymn', and the Reverend Dr John Rippon who died in 1836 leaving six volumes of hand-written inscriptions copied by him from Bunhill Fields. Such industry could be but a drop in the ocean in recording stones in a graveyard where it is thought that more than 120,000 bodies were buried. (Records, including interment books and inscriptions as at 1869 can be seen on request at the Guildhall library in the City.)

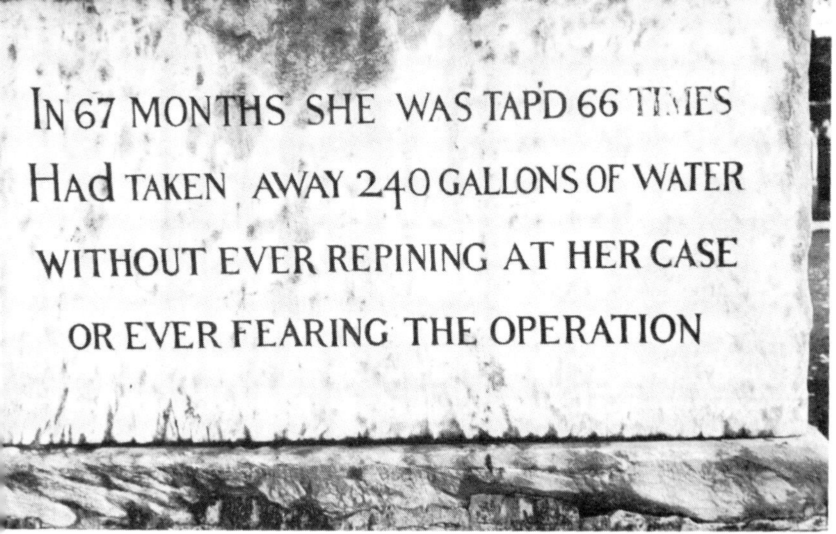

13 This inscription on the tomb of Dame Mary Page in Bunhill Fields, London, speaks for itself

Concern over the insanitary conditions of central London burial grounds led to the closure of Bunhill in 1853. Shortly before this, seven 'hygienic' cemeteries had been established away from the centre including those at Highgate, to the north – where now rest the bodies of Karl Marx, George Eliot and Christina Rossetti – and Kensal Green in the west, which contains the graves of such literary figures as Trollope, Thackeray, Francis Thompson and poet Leigh Hunt whose stone bears his own famous line, 'Write me as one who loves his fellow men'.

However the famous are commemorated, as Gray pointed out in his moving *Elegy Written in a Country Churchyard*, 'the paths of glory lead but to the grave' where all are equal, and the 'short and simple annals of the poor' recorded on plain stones are as meaningful as the most ornate monument. What grief is represented by the inscription on the tablet at St Marys, Rotherhithe, to Elizabeth Wheatley, married on 20 August 1593 who 'died the XVIII Day of September the same yeare'? What conditions produced the grave at Prestbury which contains seven children of one family who died in an eight-year period from 1839, their combined ages being a mere 69 months?

Less shocking, though no doubt equally sad for his relatives, was the death in 1750 of the same village's stonemason and parish beadle, whose stone carries the quaint rhyming inscription:

Beneath this stone lies Edward Green,
Who for cutting stone famous was seen,
But he was sent to apprehend
One Joseph Clarke of Kerridge End,
For stealing deer of Squire Downes,
When he was shot and died o' th' wounds.

Other intriguing gravestones at Prestbury are to Paul Mason of Rainow who died in 1759 aged 95 and was 'Father and Grandfather to 94 children'; to Sarah Pickford, ancestor of the famous removal company, who 'died a Bachelour in the 48 yeare of her age'; and to Margaret Evans, d. 1919:

Having born none she yet had
Many children and children's children

Even to the fourth generation
Her children arise up
And call her blessed

The mystery is solved when it is known that Margaret was nanny to the Gaskell family (Mrs Gaskell's delightful novel, *Cranford*, being based on nearby Knutsford).

Such epitaphs should be cherished while their stones remain, for it is a sad fact that many fine churches and their grounds are being allowed to decay through lack of financial or other support. Leading figures such as the Poet Laureate, Sir John Betjeman, have long waged a battle to preserve many disused churches, advocating their conversion to secular activities, as has happened with Holy Trinity, Colchester, now a museum of country life, or the breath-taking architectural grace of All Saints, Oxford, which houses Lincoln College library. The 1977 exhibition on the future of our churches, 'Change and Decay' (see Further Reading), used telling photographs to illustrate the many beautiful church buildings demolished since World War II, and those abandoned which will face a similar fate unless prompt action is taken. In the Diocese of London, for example, half of the thirty-eight churches declared redundant in 1968 have already been demolished. The same problem exists in other large cities such as Birmingham, Glasgow, Liverpool and Manchester. Country churches too are not immune, with Welsh chapels being sold off regularly and the wealth of East Anglia lying crumbling in the fields of Norfolk.

Some help is at hand, however. Such exhibitions can only do good, as can the recent British Tourist Authority report, *Chapels, Churches, Kirks: Who Cares?*. The Friends of the Friendless Churches organization also aims to preserve abandoned churches and ultimately restore them to use. They have over a hundred repaired churches to their credit, establishing local Friends groups to continue the upkeep of such buildings. At the time of writing, seven churches as far apart as Essex and South Devon are leased to them on ninety-nine year agreements for preservation as monuments, including two residual towers in Yorkshire and Lincolnshire. The little church of St Peter, Wolfhamcote, on the Warwicks/ Northants border, has lost its village and stood in a state

15 Before restoration, crumbling masonry, broken windows and gravestones leaning at perilous angles, add to the air of dereliction at the church of St Peter, Wolfhamcote

of decay for many years (illustration 15). Now splendidly restored by the Friends, it is used for occasional services. For further details write to the Hon. Director, c/o 12 Edwardes Square, London W8 6HG.

Such stemming of the tide must not lead to complacency. In some cases when churches are still used, alterations are carried out which supposedly make them more fitting to the modern world, alterations such as removing the gravestones to make room for electric mowing machines. By taking an intelligent interest in rubbings of church memorials, from the finest brass to the simplest stone, enthusiasts can play some small part in preserving and recording a vital part of our heritage.

2 What to Rub — Street Furniture

Coal Plates

Coal-hole covers are excellent subjects for rubbings, of attractive design, with a raised surface and frequently intriguing histories. Small enough to be rubbed quickly – usually about a foot in diameter – the covers are said to have been made this size to prevent easy access by burglars. As the name implies, the circular cast-iron lids set in pavements cover holes leading to cellars where coal was stored. Known in the trade as coal plates they date, in the main, from the mid-nineteenth century and are still to be found outside many houses of this period where town planners have failed to hack up the original spacious pavements for road-widening and other public utility schemes.

As well as being produced in a bewildering variety of patterns – stars, circles, squares, crosses and even 'snow flakes' – some coal plates have a series of small holes incorporated in the design, whilst others contain large sections of glass. Those with holes are early examples, so formed to enable fresh air to enter the cellar in an age when stored coal was thought to give off injurious gases. Unfortunately, Victorian ingenuity failed to take weather conditions into account when inventing these holed plates, so that rain too found them a useful access point. Solid plates were consequently introduced, only to be replaced within a short time by glass covers which enabled small patches of daylight to enter the cellars.

Indeed, illuminated pavement lights which rendered previously unused underground rooms of service, were much in vogue at the end of the nineteenth century. Framed in cast iron they were manufactured by the same iron founders who produced other public necessities – all eminently 'rubbable' – such as inspection covers, gratings and ventilation panels as well as coal plates.

Anyone with an interest in industrial archaeology can become just as 'hooked' on the story of a particular iron founder and his wares as the social historian becomes on the background to monumental brasses. But be warned, searching for unusual coal plates

16 Cast iron coal plate with snow flake design produced by a Midlands iron founder

17 Distinctive wax rubbing from the same plate (*Geoffrey Warren*)

18 Late coal plate with glass insets

with eyes constantly focussed on the ground can become almost too-engrossing a hobby when it results in mid-pavement collisions. Civilized behaviour on the sidewalk is just as important as in a churchyard.

Someone well aware of this, who still managed to find and note over 150 different coal plates in central London alone (illustrations 19 and 20) was a Victorian doctor, Shephard T. Taylor. Whilst a medical student, Taylor became obsessed by coal-hole covers. So expert was he at recognizing the different patterns, that he claimed to be able to make lightning sketches of all new ones, automatically discarding any previously noted. Hiding under the published pseudonym of Aesculapius Junior, it was Dr Taylor who coined the now accepted term for coal plates, the suitably obscure 'opercula'. Defined by the *Oxford Dictionary* as 'the lid or valve closing aperture of shell', the Latin *operculum* is indeed a most fitting word for the action of the covers and the verbose era which spawned them. It also sprang naturally from the good Doctor's scientific training, being much used by zoologists. When attempting to trace designs pinpointed by Taylor it is interesting to see how many of the streets

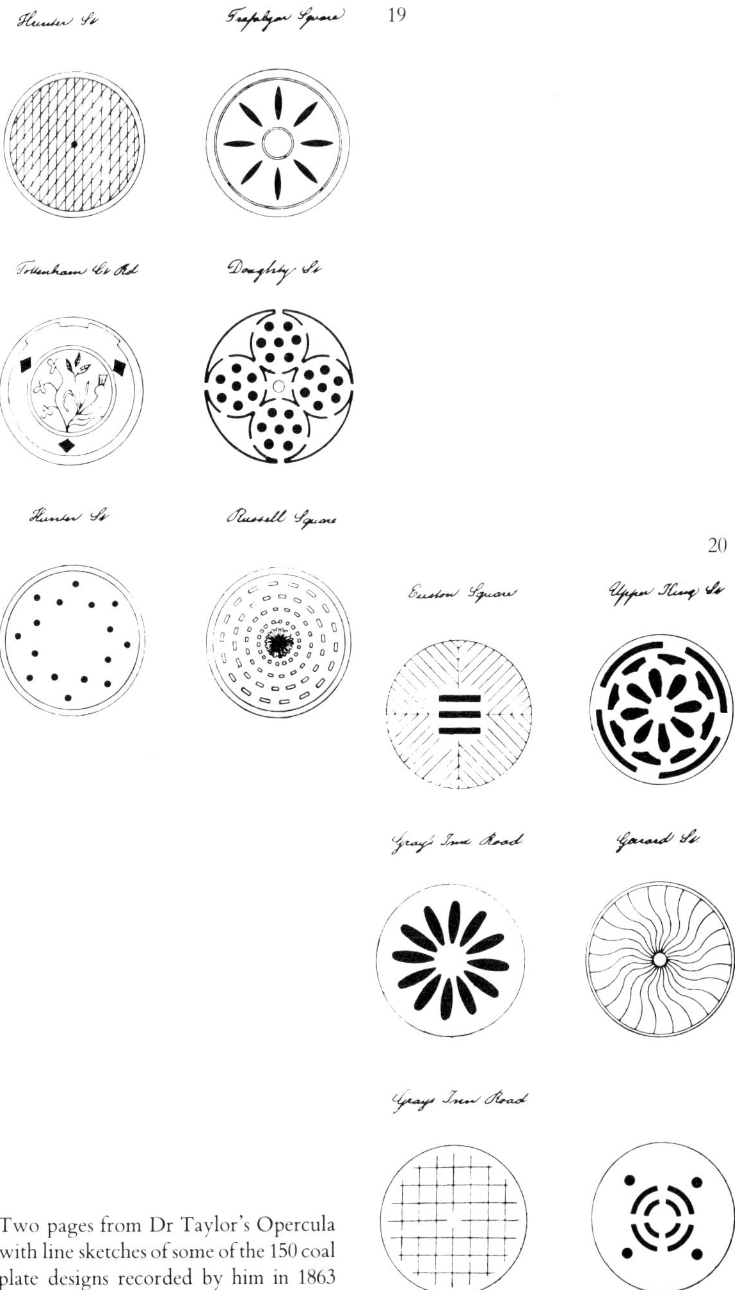

Two pages from Dr Taylor's Opercula with line sketches of some of the 150 coal plate designs recorded by him in 1863 (Museum of London)

named by him contain hospitals or other institutions where he was presumably working at the time.

Sadly many of the more delicate patterns have been worn away and in some cases pavements have disappeared altogether, so that anyone wishing to rub the same plates today might well be unable to find them. However, most older urban areas still retain a fair sprinkling of covers, many of which are attractive enough to be rubbed in their own right, although discovering their background does add a fascinating extra dimension and frequently the rubbing can preserve a real piece of history.

Dating coal plates is an uncertain business. Whilst in the majority of cases plates coincide with housing development and can be placed reasonably accurately, many cellars were added much later and a lot of plates have been replaced with the passing years. Most plates are thought to date from around 1863, the year in which Taylor made his study, but there is one outside an 1820s house in Norland Square, west London, that might be as old as the building. It is possible, however, to piece together information such as location, type of cover and other relevant features like fasteners – early plates with no fastening were highly dangerous and led to the speedy development of many self-locking protective devices – and thus gain a fairly accurate idea of when the plate was installed.

One prominent coal plate manufacturer advertised six types of plates in 1865, but such was the undesirable publicity resulting from accidents caused by dangerous plates that, by 1875, some ten new designs had been added, most illuminated and with a recommended safety chain and ring device. The injury to Sir P. C. Owen who, as reported in the *Daily Telegraph* at the time was unable to greet Queen Victoria because '. . . happening to step on an unfastened iron plate over a coal-cellar, the treacherous ground slipped aside and his leg went down the opening . . .' may seem amusing today, but was obviously quite painful. Indeed, one poor lady who fell down a coal hole in London's Russell Square died of her injuries, when it was admitted that 'three quarters of the plates in that neighbourhood were unfastened'.

Knowledge of leading manufacturers is perhaps the most useful aid in establishing the origin of particular coal plates, and often a rubbing from an idiosyncratic cover can be the start of excit-

21 Rubbing of a Haywards patent coal plate 'badged' for the retailer, H. C. Davis & Co, and proclaiming its virtues (*Geoffrey Warren*)

ing detective work beginning in museums, and leading through old directories and company histories to a branch of that same firm which may still be in existence today. Just as the bulk of brasses are to be found in those areas where there was a lack of suitable monumental stone, so the majority of coal plates were made in the traditional iron founding areas of the North and Midlands where raw materials abounded. And as each engraver and mason left their own distinctive marks on brasses and stone so too, though in an admittedly much cruder way, suiting the times and the utility of the object, did the coal-hole makers. For instance the Scots firm of Carron from Falkirk, makers of the old solid telephone kiosks, introduced the star-patterned plates. Other manufacturers put their names on the covers, several of which also demonstrated their virtues to the world, being described as 'Automatic Action' and 'Safety Plate Improved' and even 'Efficiency' and 'Durability'.

One delightful plate, the dog with its head in a pot (cover and illustration 38), the trademark of Haywards of the Borough, London SE1, will serve admirably as an example of the interesting data which can come to light when exploring the origins of a coal-hole cover rubbed, in the first instance, purely because of the appeal of the amusing design as a subject for decoration. The original wooden dog and pot, most decidedly an ancient inn sign – now in the Cuming Museum, Southwark – was known to have hung outside an ironmonger's shop as early as 1783. Noted as far back as the fifteenth century as a reproach to slovenly housewives who were too lazy to wash their pots and pans under the communal pump but simply threw them on the floor for the dogs to lick clean, the representation of hound and cooking utensil was probably taken over as appropriate by an ironmonger as he made both the dog (firedogs) and the iron pots to put over the flames.

A similar brass sign was certainly still hanging above 196 Blackfriars Road in 1823 when Charles Dickens, as a small boy, made the journey from his house in Lant Street, Southwark, to the blacking factory by Hungerford Stairs (now Charing Cross), described so graphically in *David Copperfield*. In a letter to John Forster he states

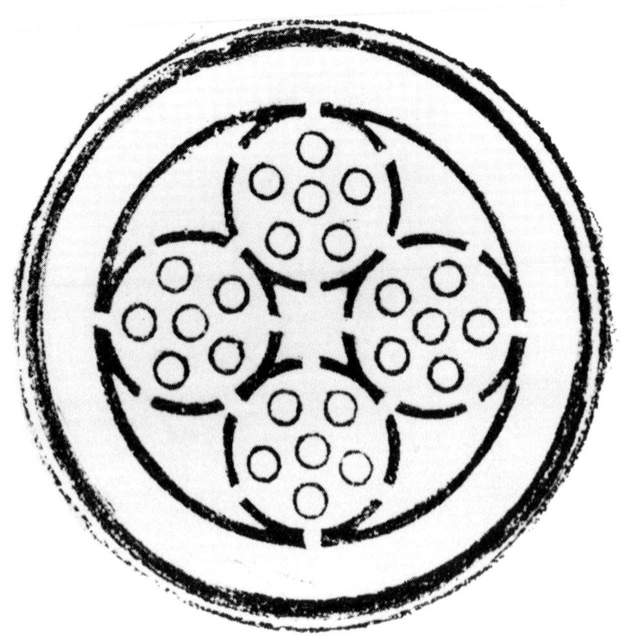

22 Ventilation holes are clearly shown in this coal plate rubbing (*Geoffrey Warren*)

that 'my usual way home' lies via 'Blackfriars Road which has Rowland Hill's chapel on one side and the likeness of a golden dog licking a golden pot over a shop door on the other'.

Haywards, famous at the time for their Patent Sheringham Ventilator which took away stale air from overcrowded rooms, took over the business in Blackfriars Road in 1849, together with a nearby foundry, and adopted the dog and pot as their own, using it on many coal plates from that time. The retail business eventually passed to J. W. Cunningham and Co. whose name can clearly be seen on the plate illustrated on page 85 which bears the date 1882. It was customary for the ironmonger supplying the plates to ask the foundry making them to imprint his own company name on the covers – known as 'badging' – as a permanent type of advertising. This name change from manufacturer to supplier can be confusing for the coal-hole cover enthusiast trying to find background information to a particular rubbing.

As is described in chapter 3 rubbing coal plates is exceedingly simple and produces excellent results as the patterns are large and bold. The basic method is exactly the same as for all negative rubbings (page 60). No one with any sense would try to rub coal-hole covers in wet or windy weather or on a busy pavement where there is constant traffic. If you are in the commercial area of a city, try to wait until the early evening when most of the crowds have gone and you can work without interruption. In a residential quarter you will always find curious children watching your efforts, but often the conversation with them is as rewarding as the actual task. Talking to any local inhabitant is a good idea: someone will put you on the track of another good example or come up with an interesting snippet of history about the area.

Forming a collection of coal plate rubbings can be of use to historical societies and schools too. One large collection entitled 'A Survey of Coal Hole covers in London' is in the Museum of London (Appendix B) and is available to the public on request. It is the result of a project carried out in 1971 and organized by the Schools Service of the old London Museum, during which thirty-two schools cooperated to rub coal-hole covers around the capital. There have also been occasional exhibitions of rubbings of plates, and the actual coal covers, when available, fetch a good price in antique shops.

Pillar Boxes, Plaques and Paraphernalia

Pillar Boxes

Once bitten by the rubbing bug you'll want to take impressions of any relief surface which catches your eye. And why not so long as they are attractive, can be put to good use or stimulate further interest? Railway buffs I know are not averse to displaying rubbings of old station signs, particularly name-plates of some favoured class of engine and other *memorabilia* of the proud age of steam. And one friend decorated the loo walls with rubbings of old brass trade plates and other intriguing signs which helped keep the occupants of the smallest room amused!

One idea which sprang out of the London schools coal plate rubbing project was to trace postal history through making rubbings of the various royal ciphers found on pillar boxes (illustration 23). Of course, there is now no remaining sign of William Dockwra's first, unofficial Penny Post for London, introduced in 1680 to receive and deliver from hundreds of specially set up offices. And obviously there are only written and pictorial records of the bell men who paraded the streets on post nights to collect and carry mail to the General Post Office till as late as 1846. Those interested in early examples of main post boxes can, however, still see what is believed to be the oldest post office letter box in existence, now in Wakefield museum, Yorks, and dating from its erection in that town in 1809.

Fortunately too, there are many surviving old free-standing pillar boxes, including some dating from 1853, the first boxes to be installed throughout the country after the introduction of a uniform Penny Post in 1840. Indeed, it is believed that one remaining box at St Peter port, Guernsey, may well be one of the original prototype boxes put up as early as 1851 when the novelist Anthony Trollope, then a Post Office surveyor's clerk, was sent to the Channel Isles to study ways of improving their postal service and recommended following the French method of 'fitting up letter boxes in posts fixed at the road side'. It is intriguing to note that this box, now protected by iron railings, carries a cipher proper to the reign of William IV.

Very early mainland boxes can still be tracked down in country districts such as Barnes Cross, Bishop's Caundle, Dorset – an

23 Rubbings of royal ciphers on pillar boxes from Victoria to the present Queen, by children of the Lower Latymer Junior School, Enfield. Note the rare Edward VIII cipher (*Museum of London*)

octagonal shape with a vertical posting aperture – and on the Framlingham Road in Suffolk. During the first four years the choice of box, its design and manufacture was in the hands of the local District Surveyor which resulted in many differing types. Country pillar boxes were finally standardized in 1857 following the first six 'standard' rectangular boxes introduced in London two years earlier on Rowland Hill's recommendation. Boxes at sub-post offices, however, continued to be provided at the expense of the sub-postmaster and were usually made by a local carpenter.

Perhaps the most appealing pillar boxes still to be seen today are the hexagonal shaped ones (illustration 24) which were used from 1866–79 and are commonly referred to as 'Penfolds' after the architect and surveyor who designed them. Later boxes were circular, fluted, conical and flat-roofed, first being painted the now-established red colour just over a hundred years ago in 1874. The 1880s revealed a slip in the Post Office memory bank when someone forgot to put its name on boxes issued at that time in London, nor was the royal cipher used, so that a series of 'anonymous' boxes still remain in the capital and in Liverpool.

Postal historians also point to the rarity of boxes bearing the cipher of Edward VIII, the uncrowned king. Before the abdication some 271 boxes containing his cipher were made (illustration 23), but many were later changed to George VI so that only one hundred or so boxes thus marked still remain.

Facts about old boxes were few until some fifteen years ago. In 1964, for instance, only twenty-eight early boxes were recorded. Then, through the *Post Office Magazine* Treasure Hunt, readers were invited to submit examples of boxes in their districts. The search was enthusiastically backed by the media, producing an excellent response, with all submissions being checked out by local postal workers. Results of the survey, together with many photographic illustrations and line drawings of different types of boxes, are included in Jean Young Farrugia's detailed history of pillar and wall boxes, *The Letter Box* (see Further Reading).

Fire Marks

Another commonly accepted service which also originated in 1680 was fire insurance, when Dr Nicholas Barbon's 'Fire Office' – the

24 Victorian hexagonal Penfold pillar box still in use

first fire insurance company in the world – was set up and adopted the sign of a phoenix rising from the flames (the 'Phenix Office' name was adopted in 1705). Other early fire protection offices were the 'Friendly Society of London' (1683), the 'Hand-in-Hand' (1696), the 'Sun' (1710) and the 'Union' (1714).

Those with but a passing interest in fire-fighting itself, cannot fail to be intrigued by the fire marks issued by the insuring companies and still to be seen on some protected buildings today. Made of metal, the plates which bore the company's insignia, were fixed to the front of the insured building, usually between the first-floor windows. The very decorative and highly individual marks indicated that the property was securely insured and were thus a deterrent to fraudulent firms which tried to claim insurance after a fire but had no proof of cover.

In the days of few fixed addresses, fire marks also helped confirm that a policy did relate to a particular property as well as helping guide the office fire brigade to the burning building. Self-advertisement by the competing insurance companies was another later use of fire marks. Early marks up to about 1800 were usually

25 Plaque to commemorate the Elizabethan Fortune Theatre

made of lead and contained the actual policy number, a true source of identification, whereas the iron and tin plates from 1820–25 mainly served as advertisements.

Whilst fire marks produce attractive rubbings, the enthusiast may experience difficulty in discovering old ones still in place outside buildings and many have disappeared as ancient offices have been pulled down or replaced. Anyone wishing to explore the subject further would do well to visit the Chartered Insurance Institute, Aldermanbury, in the City of London, which contains the most comprehensive collection of British fire marks in the world, and also has many continental plates on display. Marks included range from a rare 1680s 'Friendly Society of London' sign – a sheaf of arrows with

26 The Fortune Theatre in its heyday from a print published by Wilkinson in 1811

entwined serpent, through a distinctive wool trade town, the 'Leeds Fire Office' – ram with three stars above – about one hundred years later, to the porcelain blue and white plaques of the old 'Athenaeum Fire Insurance Office' of the 1850s.

Blue Plaques

London's famous blue commemorative plates, of which there are still less than 400, provide another fascinating source of study. Very few people will be interested in *all* the famous men and women and the buildings associated with them recorded in this way. Yet a student of English literature may well wish to establish a collection of plaques, in photographs, drawings, rubbings and notes of the eminent dramatists, novelists, poets and men of letters who have made their mark on the London literary scene, from 1866 when the Royal Society of Arts put up the first terracotta plate outside Byron's residence at 24 Holles Street, to the plate to Virginia Woolf, nearly one hundred years later at 29 Fitzroy Square, Camden. Followers of such diverse life-styles as those of the armed forces, cartoonists, philosophers and scientists, will also find much to stimulate them on plaques from Barnet to Westminster.

Commemorative plaques are not, of course, confined to London, with many historical societies indicating buildings of interest, either architecturally or historically, by some type of decorative tablet (illustration 25). Again, if wishing to rub such a stone or bronze plate it is essential to obtain permission first. And do remember that,

being fixed high up on house fronts or level with street names, plaques are difficult to reach.

Recent blue plaques erected on buildings occupied by such non-establishment figures as Marie Lloyd, the music hall artiste and Donald McGill, the saucy postcard illustrator, have caused some controversy. Should you know of a building of some historic interest which has connections with a notable London figure and feel that this association is worth recording, then write with the reasons for your suggestion to the Surveyor of Historic Buildings, Greater London Council, County Hall, SE1.

3 How to Rub

Anyone can make a successful rubbing. People who happily admit to having no artistic talent can, with a minimum of instruction and a little experience, create eye-catching rubbings which are marvellous for display and whose history provides a ready talking point. Once hooked, the dedicated rubber will want to take impressions of all types of relief surfaces, happily delving into their respective backgrounds. It is probably best however to concentrate on one subject initially, to learn all there is to know about making such rubbings and then apply the various techniques to whatever takes your fancy.

As *brass* rubbings are the most popular kind, especially now that the rubbing centres have made brasses more easily available in facsimile, the following information on materials and methods is based, in the main, on rubbing brasses. However, the beauty of making rubbings is that the same basic skills and procedures apply whatever the object to be rubbed. Wherever a different type of paper, tool or technique is required, for say stone or cast iron, these are described separately.

First decide on the brass to be rubbed. As stated previously, anyone living within reach of a brass rubbing centre (Appendix C) will have an excellent opportunity to learn how to rub, with materials usually provided and up to seventy brasses on which to work for a small fee. After reaching some degree of proficiency and arming yourself with the necessary materials, you will be ready to move on to a church brass. The country's top thirty churches with brasses are given in Appendix D. A detailed list of London churches containing brasses will be found in Appendix F and a more general countrywide selection of outstanding brasses in Appendix E.

However, not all of the brasses noted are available for rubbing. In some cases, mainly because of frailty, brasses are housed behind glass. In others, they have been removed from their original positions on the church floor and repositioned far above human reach. And in some parishes the policy of the church is simply opposed to brass rubbing.

There is little point, therefore, in turning up unannounced at a church of your choice and expecting to be able to rub the brasses. Do make prior enquiry. A phone call, or preferably a letter to the local vicar, will soon establish his views on brass rubbing and a suitable appointment may be made. If the desired brass lies within a university college or similar institution then the same approach should be made to the relevant authority. Likewise, do consult the vicar if you want to rub a gravestone, however old. He will be able to tell you whether there are relatives of the dead who may object to someone trampling around the grave and wearing away at the stone. And, if a coal plate or other cover is outside a private house, then take the precaution of making sure that the householder does not object to your activity, even if the pavement containing the cover is so-called public property.

It may sound over-cautious to go to such lengths in obtaining permission to rub, but a little courtesy and foreknowledge does no one any harm and may prevent complications all round. Many people, for instance, plan their brass rubbing expeditions for weekends when they are not working and the children are not at school. They forget that this is often the clergy's busiest time, with Saturday weddings and services throughout Sunday when it is impossible to allow brass rubbing. And remember that tourists, particularly those from the United States with a whirlwind once-in-a-lifetime itinerary, will often have booked months ahead so that summertime appointments at certain churches are not easy to obtain.

Does the church charge for brass rubbing? Some churches where there are famous brasses have a printed scale of fees. Others ask small charges to be paid to the vicar or verger, while many do not state specific sums but merely remind brass rubbers that they are in a house of God and to keep the place tidy. In this latter case I usually put whatever can be afforded into the offertory box.

Materials

Paper and wax are the only two indispensable rubbing materials. The degree of sophistication of either depends on how seriously the art of rubbing is taken. Let us merely say that it *is* possible to make rubbings with most types of paper and wax, but the results will not be anywhere near as spectacular or long-lasting as those done with the recommended materials, some of which are produced especially for rubbing and have been proved over many years.

Wax crayons for instance can be used, but the rubbing will lack depth and will smudge easily. It will also fade in time. The ideal consistency is found in heelball, cobbler's wax, obtainable through most shoe-menders. Shops selling art and crafts materials also supply heelball, but the best quality, made especially for brass rubbing is that produced by Phillips & Page, 50 Kensington Church Street, London W8 (Appendix A), who specialize in anything and everything to do with rubbing brasses.

This heelball is very hard and produces a good shine. It is supplied in many colours, such as white, green and blue, as well as the conventional black. There is also a metallic gold, silver and bronze, slightly more expensive but producing beautiful results when rubbed up to an overall sheen. Heelball comes in sticks – a little thicker than the usual wax crayons and easier to hold – and cakes about the size of a bar of soap. Sticks are best for brasses, particularly small ones with delicate lines, as they allow more control. Cakes make rubbing large surfaces easier, especially crude ones of cast iron like coal plates where a lot of force and more expansive movements are necessary.

All experienced rubbers have their own favourite papers, some of which will be described in more detail in the next chapter. In general, for a negative – black wax on white paper – rubbing, ordinary lining paper available from wallpaper shops is perfectly acceptable. Such paper, perfect for beginners who do not wish to spend too much in case they do not take to rubbing, has the necessary strength to take the pressure of rubbing but is thin enough to produce a good impression of the brass beneath. It does tend to yellow with age which many find acceptable as opposed to the hard white of some papers.

One particularly white paper, perhaps the most widely recommended for rubbing, is architects' detail paper which has just the right combination of strength and delicacy. Available from good stationers and specialist shops, it also has the advantage of being supplied in different widths, particularly useful for the larger brasses. But it is expensive, coming in 50-yard rolls, can be unwieldy and often results in wastage when used on smaller brasses. Until you have an idea of how much rubbing will be done in the future, it may be advisable to buy smaller amounts of one or two papers rather than the big roll, especially as a lighter grade paper is needed for later brasses with fine lines.

Also necessary (illustration 27) are a duster to clean the brass and another soft cloth, preferably a nylon stocking or tights, to polish up the rubbing. Some people take along a hand-brush to make sure that the stone is really free from dirt, but even the lightest scraping might harm the brass so brushing cannot be recommended. This is equally true of tombs and gravestones. Even though a churchyard stone may be lichen-encrusted do not be tempted to use a brush to remove it. Rubbing with a rag will take away most surface dirt and vegetation, and an eraser should soon get rid of any hard patches of green or grey discolouration which are found in nooks and crannies.

The only occasion when a brush is useful, indeed indispensable, is when preparing to rub a coal plate or other pavement cover. A good scrub with a stiff brush cannot harm the plate and will get rid of any accumulated dirt which might otherwise tear the paper. Look for clearly-defined plates where the pattern or lettering has not been worn away and where the iron is still intact, not filled in with lumps of concrete. Avoid plates playing host to seemingly innocent materials which the brush fails to dislodge; chewing gum, for example, may have set apparently solid but will play havoc with the paper as soon as any pressure is put on it.

Masking tape is also needed to hold the paper in place. The cellulose tape is equally adhesive, almost too much so, marking stone and peeling off whitewash from walls, so should be avoided. Scissors make life easier when cutting paper, and take something to kneel on, like an old sweater – hassocks, when available, are very comfortable and useful for weighing down the paper.

Basic Method

First find your brass. Many of them are not instantly visible, often being hidden under carpet or matting. Others may have been moved from the floor to a more secure position on a wall, while some are to be found in such unconventional places as on the font, in the doorway, or on exterior walls or in the churchyard.

Do not start to work immediately but spend a few minutes simply

27 Equipment for rubbing, showing white and coloured papers, sticks and cakes of heelball, masking tape and dusters

looking at the brass, absorbing its detail and, if you know anything of the person thus commemorated, thinking back to their life and times. Then, if you are wearing strong shoes, take them off so as not to damage the stone or even, inadvertently, tread on the brass. Rubbing enthusiasts can hardly be asked to take warm slippers with them everywhere, but frozen toes are not much fun either so try to carry a pair of woollen socks or wear rubber-soled shoes.

Carefully clean the brass with a soft cloth making sure that all dust and dirt is removed. If you intend to leave the rubbing on its original paper then care must be taken to ensure that the stone is clean too as the smallest piece of grit can easily make a tear which will spoil the whole effect. Disciples of rubbing facsimile brasses would here point out that no such elaborate preventative measures need be taken with reproductions which hang up in clean surroundings when not in use and, possibly more important, are light enough to be moved about at will and positioned on tables as well as floors so that the person rubbing need not suffer from housemaid's knee or back-ache. Valid points, especially for older people, but what chance do they have against the sense of mystery which is everywhere when rubbing in churches.

It is important to take another good long look at the brass to fix it in the mind, especially since if you intend keeping the same paper, you cannot afford to go over the edges with the wax. A picture of the brass is a good idea so that you can consult it when working on difficult areas. If time allows, it is preferable to take a rough, light rubbing first, then prop it in a convenient place for reference as you do the rubbing proper.

Next position the paper as centrally as possible over the brass and secure it with tape, hassocks, etc. Make sure that the paper is as tight as can be for it is impossible to gain a clear impression on rippling paper. If the brass is very large, as the armoured knights often are – a good 6ft tall and nearly a yard wide – then the widest paper must be used. Joins can be made and do not appear to detract from the rubbing when it is still on the brass, but making a good, permanent join later requires time and patience. All too often good rubbings are spoiled by bubbly lines across the middle.

Securing paper on wall brasses is as difficult as it is to rub them successfully. Four hands make light the work of two, but I would never advise anyone to volunteer to hold the paper in position for any length of time, especially above the head which is a real form of torture. Tape can be attached to marble or slate as it can to any stone but will not stick to plaster without there being a strong chance of the paint coming away with the adhesive when the rubbing is completed.

Many mural brasses are in 'frames', a stone setting shaped to look like other memorial tablets and fixed to the walls by studs. These have to be rubbed most carefully as it is not easy to position the paper correctly over the frequently sloping 'shoulders' of the frame. Some experienced rubbers advise taking a sheet of paper large enough to cover the whole stone and folding it at a point where the carving begins, then fixing it only to that point, on the straight edges of the frame as it were, so long as all major parts of the brass lie under the secured part. Holding the flap of paper out of the way – again an assistant is very necessary – rub the section under the taped paper, then unfold the flap and rub the final part, keeping the paper in position with one hand and rubbing with the other. Difficult, but possible, and usually well worth the effort to gain an unusual brass. But do not balance precariously on unsuitable pew ends or benches to rub such brasses. Find a solid chair at least. If someone connected with the building is on the spot then ask what they would recommend. One kind verger even fetched me a step stool, though I have known others who made it patently clear that rubbing such oddly-positioned brasses was not encouraged.

Securing paper out of doors is frequently troublesome. On pavements, tape does stick to the stone, but there are often minute dirt particles which cause it to come unstuck at just the wrong moment. A sudden draught caused by wind blowing down an alley or a lorry hurtling by will also whip up the tape without warning. It may sound lazy but I prefer to drive to interesting coal plates with a load of hefty books or even bricks in the car to ensure that the paper remains fixed. Kneeling on one edge of the paper is also a good idea and I've never torn a rubbing by this heavyweight method although I have by trying to save paper unstuck by the elements.

Shaped gravestones present probably the greatest problem of all as it is almost impossible to secure paper to the sometimes crumbly, often damp stone. A table tomb is relatively simple, as again weights can be used on the flat surface where tape will not stick. And as with wall brasses, good quality stone, marble and slate present few problems. It is essential to have the correct size of paper for a shaped stone: I have wrestled in vain with too-large rolls, cutting off sheets of the correct length but failing to secure the extra width with any degree of success. Take just enough paper to overlap the stone at the top and on both sides, then tape it as firmly as possible to the back of the stone, first at both corners, pleating it a little behind to achieve a snug fit at the front, and then across the top and down the sides. It is preferable to cut the paper from the roll at the bottom too as there is nothing more ruinous to good quality paper than lying in wet grass or on dirty earth, and it does need to be positioned as tightly as possible to secure a good impression.

With the paper in place go round the outline of the brass or inscription with a finger so that the edges stand out; this will help prevent rubbing over them. However careful you are, it is all too easy to stray over the edges, particularly for beginners, so many people hold a piece of card against the edges to capture any erring wax. This always seems an unnecessary chore and as I usually cut out and mount rubbings anyway (Chapter 5) I generally rub over the edges – the stone setting can make quite an attractive background in itself. For those who try not to mark the paper but make the occasional error, there is an eraser which will get rid of most small traces of wax, which is available at most rubbing centres.

Start to rub. Do not be carried away by seeing the lines of the brass revealed so that you hasten to complete the rubbing as quickly as possible. Take your time and rub only in sections. It is usually best to start at the top of the brass and work down, moving on to another section only when you feel you have achieved the best possible result on the previous one. Some prefer to reveal the major lines of the brass first, then gradually bring out the detail, but this method is fatal if the paper moves and different areas are superimposed on each other, if only by a fraction, so that blurred lines result. Paper often stretches when being rubbed so I would always recommend the sectionalized approach rather than going for the grand design, which is where the rough outline rubbing for reference comes in useful.

Rub hard to make the incised lines stand out and achieve a strong uniform colour. And always rub in the same direction. Nothing looks uglier than lots of lines going every which way in an attempt to form a solid background. If in doubt about this, practise like schoolchildren do on a coin. Messy rubbing may produce an impression but not a clear one.

Apply the same amount of pressure to the heelball at all times. You will find that a cake is most suited to the bold lines of the large early brasses and can be used over quite large areas at a time. The finer engraving of later brasses responds best to smaller, rounded pieces of heelball, while a more pointed stick brings out the really fine lines.

If rubbing gravestones with heelball, again the rounded small

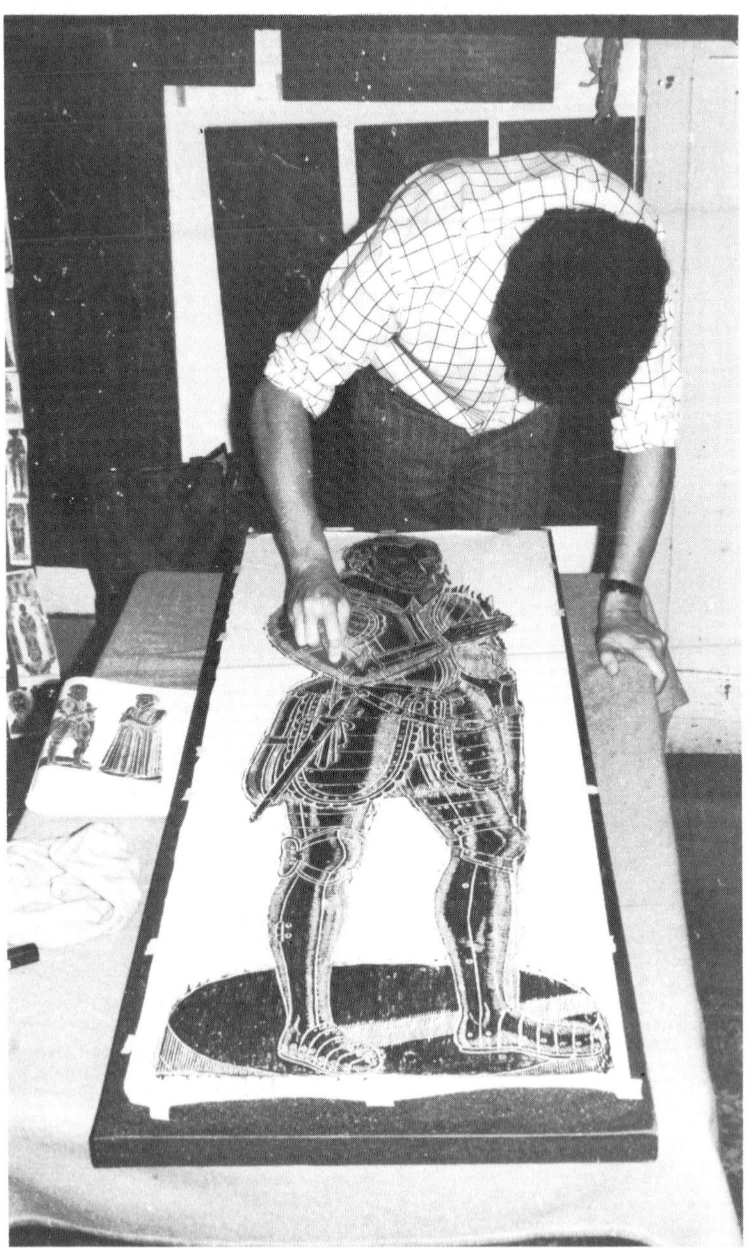

28 An almost completed rubbing with a good dark image, but the wax has strayed over the edges of the brass in several places

29 Rubbing still in position over a coal plate. In some cases, as here, the stone surround also produces an attractive pattern

pieces will make the best of the worn lines of inscriptions. By contrast, the hard cast iron of coal plates demands hard work with an equally hard cake of heelball, black or brick-red for the happiest effect.

When the rubbing is finished, scrutinize it carefully to see that no part has been missed and that it is of the same solid colour throughout. If satisfied, take the piece of nylon and polish the surface till it shines. I stumbled on the old stocking idea more by luck than judgement and was interested to see how many other rubbing enthusiasts recommend it. I have been much amused too by the curiosity of people who watched me rubbing but seemed more concerned with the pair of laddered tights lying around than with my efforts. As one American lady delicately put it, 'Pardon me, but what's the significance of the nylon hose?'!

If the brass has a missing canopy or inscription the indents can be rubbed though, as already mentioned, these are only absolutely necessary if making rubbings for the record rather than for decoration. For whatever purpose the rubbing is being taken, it is always wise to make a note of the brass with as much detail as possible. I bitterly regret having given away many rubbings without keeping a list of their brasses, and even in very early days forgetting to put down the name of the church, imagining at the time that I would always be able to recall it.

Note first the church, its dedication and geographical location, then the position of the brass in the church. Identify the subject of the brass and the approximate date of death, indicating lost parts or any not rubbed by you. Finally, 'sign' the rubbing with your name and date. Such little flourishes may seem somewhat unnecessary for something destined to be a wall hanging, but if the brass is of worth you will want to record it and if the rubbing is a good one you should be proud to put your name too it. Remember too, that even if it serves its purpose over many years to end up eventually in an attic, it may well be found at a later date and be of some additional use in starting succeeding generations on the trail of brasses and brass rubbings.

Do not despair if you have not rubbed hard enough to produce a really outstanding rubbing. Practice, as usual, goes a long way to achieving good results. And, if you still come away with greyish impressions don't just make do and put inferior rubbings on your wall, work on them at home as shown on page 77—but don't tell the purists.

The basic rubbing described above, dark wax on white paper, is known as a negative rubbing. The brass comes out looking as an undeveloped film does, with the true light areas appearing dark and the really black, etched in lines coming out white. How to make a positive rubbing, closer to the actual brass, is detailed in the next chapter along with other techniques for rubbings with a difference.

4 Different Techniques

Positive Rubbings

Accurate as the black on white negative rubbings are, they bear little resemblance to the brass as seen on the stone, its predominant colour being a dull bronze with the engraved lines showing up darkly. One way of making a so-called positive rubbing is to use a metallic bronze wax on black paper. Closer to the original in that the dense areas and the lines are revealed as on the brass, such reproductions seem to fall between two stools, failing to create the exact impression of the brass and lacking the crisp outlines of the black and white rubbings. However, gold and silver heelball on black or grey paper does make very attractive rubbings for decoration.

Another method of making a positive rubbing which has a nice antique look about it is to use white wax—there is a special colourless heelball, and candle wax is also effective when experimenting with this technique – on white paper. Rub in the usual way, tackling small areas and polishing them up with nylon as each section is finished. In poor light it is difficult to make sure that all the brass has been rubbed, but by bringing your eyes level with the surface of the paper you should be able to pick out the wax sheen and see if any parts have been overlooked.

Take up the rubbing and carry it carefully home. I usually roll new rubbings lightly round my roll of detail paper, but it is also possible to buy cardboard tubes in which to place the finished work, and these do make sure of preventing creases or tears particularly if you have to go long distances. At home, lay the rubbing out flat on a large table or an even floor, making sure that the work surface is suitably covered with newspapers or an old cloth. You can tape the rubbing down but it is just as easy to keep it flat by putting heavy weights, such as books, round the edge of the paper.

Soak a sponge in water till it is good and moist then dip it into a saucer of black Indian or printer's ink. With light, swift movements, go over the rubbing with the inked sponge. As the ink penetrates those lines not coated with wax it will fill in as a dark background and reveal an irovy-shade figure (illustration 31). Wipe off excess ink

30 A family affair: Wil Seegers, his wife and two daughters from Vossem, near Brussels, work together with silver wax on dark paper at a rubbing centre

with blotting paper or a paper handkerchief, then allow the rubbing to dry. Finally wipe over the wax figure with a damp cloth.

Black liquid shoe polish can be used instead of ink but this is sometimes too runny. Buy the kind with its own sponge applicator which helps give an even effect. It is also possible to paint over a white wax rubbing using water colours which creates a very pretty soft background. Ensure that your brush strokes are all made in the same direction.

Dabbing

Rubbing with heelball is accepted as the best way of taking impressions of most brasses, but there are occasions when the brass is so worn or the engraving so fine that the heavy wax fails to pick out the thin lines. In such cases another technique known as dabbing should be used. Dabbing is particularly effective for reproducing gravestone figures or inscriptions as it brings out the full texture of the stone with all its blemishes as well as incisions. It is also the method used by those sufficiently interested to record casements – the actual stone and indent(s) of brasses which no longer exist.

Make a dabber from cotton wool and chamois leather. Form the wool into a ball large enough to be held comfortably in the palm of the hand. Old rags torn into thin strips can be put in the middle of the ball if you don't have enough cotton wool. Then wrap the chamois leather round the ball making sure that the ends are tied firmly together.

Prepare the dabbing paste by mixing a few drops of oil with powdered graphite. Pure olive oil is expensive but is the best. Linseed oil, raw not boiled, is a cheaper substitute but thicker. Both have the advantage of being readily obtainable. Unfortunately, this does not seem to be the case with powdered graphite which is said to be sold by some chemists (as plombagine) but is more likely to be found at a good locksmith's. It took several calls over a period of time before I was able to track any down recently, so do stock up well in advance of when you wish to do the dabbing or you might be thwarted at the last minute.

Mix the oil and graphite on a piece of thick card or hardboard until it forms a dry paste. Spread it out evenly on the card in a thin layer. Pat the chamois pad on the paste until some of the mixture has

31 Positive rubbing of the brass to Sir John Foljambe, Tideswell, mounted on dark green hessian wall covering

32 Rice paper dabbing from a Thai temple mounted on hardboard and hung as a picture

been absorbed then rub it up and down on a clean part of the board to ensure an even distribution.

Cover the stone or other object with thin paper and hold it in place with masking tape. Tissue paper is best for dabbing or a thin but strong rice paper. You may need to experiment here as some of the rice papers are too 'hairy' to pick up detail on stone for which a light, smooth-textured paper is preferable. Take extra care when covering stone with tissue as it tears all too easily, a point which must also be remembered when removing the completed dabbing.

Then take up the primed dabber and dab some of the paste onto the paper, gradually working over the whole surface. Use a dabbing movement only, as rubbing will shift the paper and destroy the whole effect. Because of this a large stone could take a long time to dab. Be patient and try to achieve an even finish.

Dabbings are grey in colour, very different from the hard black wax rubbings. However, they can be equally effective, some think more so in that they do take a more accurate impression and the subdued colouring is perhaps more aesthetically appealing. Dabbing brasses must be done with great care as the oil from the pad could come through and leave a residue which would damage the next rubbing. If you gain permission to dab then please make sure that the brass is wiped clean and *dry* afterwards.

For minute detail on brasses, or if dabbing a composition of leaves or other delicate objects, substitute a finger dabber for the pad. Simply wrap a little chamois leather round the index finger and coat with paste in the usual way. You will have more control and be able to gain a sharper outline.

Another dabbing method involves the paper being dampened with a sponge and pressed firmly into the stone then dabbed gently with an inked pad. This is a simplistic way of describing the technique recommended by William McGeer in his excellent little paperback, *Reproducing Relief Surfaces* (see Further Reading). Special kits for this kind of dabbing are available in the USA through art shops but I have yet to find one in the UK. Also, I must admit to having had little success with my own version of this method, either over-inking the pad or becoming exasperated with paper which dries out too quickly. However, Mr McGeer advocates this type of dabbing as being 'up to ten times faster than rubbing' and says that 'In half an hour I once completed twelve dabbings'. I shall continue to experiment. If anyone devises a successful home-made version of such dabbing then I'd be pleased to hear of it.

Printing

Such a method is not suitable for use on brasses in that the object to be rubbed has to be thoroughly wetted. It is, however, close to that used by Sir John Cullum and Craven Ord in the eighteenth century when making their collection of over 200 copies of brasses, now in the British Museum (Appendix B). Travelling throughout the country, though concentrating mainly on East Anglia, the two men employed the curious procedure of inking the brass, wiping it clean, laying on damp paper covered by a cloth and simply walking all over it! The 'rubbings' were later gone over again with printer's ink, cut out and mounted in portfolios. Charming as this method sounds, such indiscriminate inking of the brasses would hardly be accepted today.

There is no reason, however, why a similar technique should not be used on coal plates although many people might be put off by the thought of flinging ink about in the great outdoors. For this type of reproduction it is best to use black printing ink and a rubber roller. The simplest method, which *can* be used on brasses as it does not entail inking the actual object, is to tape down the paper in the usual way then go over it with a well-inked roller. The design which appears will be a solid black as opposed to the grey dabbings but, of course, it will not have the shine of wax rubbings.

In the 1971 London schools survey of coal plates (page 45) some classes went even further and printed on materials by a method which did involve spreading ink on the actual cover. Here is how the then ten-year-old Mario Omar of Princess May Primary School, described his school's activities:

> First we cleaned the plate thoroughly with a wire brush then we got clean paper to spred on the table then we got the coal cover and the oil printing ink and roller we Squeezed the oil printing ink on the coal cover and got the roller and rolled it all over the cover it only went on the raised part of the design then we got the T-Shirt or apron or Skirt then we put the T-Shirt on the coal cover then we got the clean roller and started to roll the Shirt and the design got on the Shirt then we took it off and made it dry two or three days.

His spelling may be shaky and his punctuation non-existent but the method is perfectly sound and was obviously enjoyed by that group, at least.

Fabrics and Foil

All the methods previously described are suited to fabric as well as paper, though requiring slightly different techniques. Not all materials take easily to every method. Cotton and linen are most suitable for wax rubbings, while silk or muslin are best for dabbing. For printing, cotton is again the most receptive fabric.

The problem with using any type of material is that it will stretch and no matter how firmly you tape it down, if untreated in any way, it will move and thus distort the design. Always hold the fabric

33 Child's rubbing on a T-shirt. As the material was not stiffened and the rubber did not press very hard the figure is rather faint

firmly in place over the object, and rub small sections at a time preferably between the thumb and index finger of the hand which is holding down the material.

One way of making sure that fabric does not stretch is to starch it before use. Remember to rub the side which has *not* been starched. The resultant rubbing, done in exactly the same way as a conventional negative brass rubbing, will look equally attractive. It can be fixed by lightly ironing the other side of the fabric, but do not remove the starch as this could harm the wax and produce a limp rubbing which would be difficult to mount.

Fabric rubbings are best hung on the wall – a six-foot armed man rubbed directly onto a coloured linen background looks most impressive. Indeed, very little else can be done with starched wax rubbings which cannot be washed, although for a brief period one girl proudly wore what she called 'an original work of art' for special occasions, this being a long cotton skirt with rubbings of coal plates all over it. And, if you want to keep the children busy then give them old T-shirts and let them rub away to their heart's content (illustration 33). Children are also happy making rubbings on old sheets and other pieces of discarded material which might serve as temporary bed-covers or be cut out and sewn to provide dressing-up clothes.

Enterprising people have been known to make very light rubbings of intricate figures for use as embroidery patterns. A medieval figure woven into a tapestry chair back or seat can look very effective, although I would draw the line at the suggestion of two visitors to the London Museum who were anxious to obtain templates from sewer covers as they wished to crochet lavatory seat covers in the same design!

Aluminium foil is an excellent rubbing material, producing some really spectacular designs. But first a word of warning. Although, when worked up, it gives startlingly realistic reproduction of brasses, it should not be used for this purpose. Pressing on the foil to bring out the lines of the brass could well cause damage to the original. If, for some reason, you might wish to have one unusual brass, say for exhibition purposes, then ask at one of the rubbing centres if you can use foil on a facsimile, although do not be surprised if they are not happy with the idea.

Foil can be used with impunity though on coal plates and to take impressions from high relief surfaces on gravestones. Kitchen foil is quite adequate for most purposes although a thicker foil, obtainable from art shops, may be used on coal-hole covers. Beware of the heavy duty patterned foils sold as wrapping materials. These do not respond to conventional foil rubbing techniques and may result in a wasted outlay, though they do accept wax which produces rather messy impressions.

Taking care not to crease the foil, fix it with tape over the object to be rubbed. Now comes the simplest and most rewarding part. Scrub with a stiff nailbrush over the plate or stone and immediately the pattern will spring out of the foil (illustration 34). You will find that an old toothbrush is useful for getting into corners and the handle can be used to press out the lines with greater force. Prise the rubbing from the plate, taking great care not to rip it if the lines are deeply etched, especially if it is a windy day. If you have to go any distance on foot or by public transport then wrap the rubbing round a cardboard tube and unwind it as soon as you are home. Do not place a foil rubbing *inside* such a container as it is almost impossible to

34 Using a nail brush to make a foil rubbing of a coal plate

get it out without creasing, unless you cut open the tube which is pretty wasteful if you are in the habit of making lots of foil rubbings. Again, if possible, the ideal method of transport is to lay the rubbing flat on a car seat. Some people use two large sheets of hardboard taped together at one end, but the slightest pressure can flatten out the foil and you will lose the impression.

Foil rubbings cannot be left in their original state but need strengthening for display purposes. One way to do this is to put the rubbing face down on a flat surface and go over it several times with some preserving substance. Waterglass, used before the days of 'fridges as an egg preserver, fulfils this function well, although it is difficult to find today. An old-fashioned chemist is most likely to stock it. Take care not to use too much at a time and do let each coat harden before applying the next. This requires a lot of patience. I ruined a very attractive foil rubbing by not allowing the various coats to dry and ended up with a soggy, glutinous mess full of so many creases that the pattern was virtually unrecognizable.

One method of making sure that the impression stands out and, at the same time gives the necessary weight, is to squeeze a little cellulose filler, such as 'Polyfilla' into the recessed areas on the back of the foil. A wallpaper paste such as 'Polycell' which I use for mounting rubbings (page 83) is also effective to strengthen the foil instead of the stronger waterglass.

When the backing is hard and dry, work on the face of the foil by going over it gently with a brush dipped in Indian ink or with liquid shoeshine. Again allow it to dry, then remove any excess ink by going over the flat parts with steel wool. This leaves a quite garish outline with the black, inked-in lines standing out by contrast. In some cases it is preferable to go over the whole surface very thoroughly with the steel wool which produces a softer, 'antique' effect. Foil rubbings can be cut out and mounted but this is a matter of personal choice.

William McGeer also describes how to use foil in making plaster casts of gravestone rubbings, etc, and students interested in taking the use of this medium any further are recommended to read his book. He has devised the name 'foil daubings' for a process which involves wiping metallic paste onto painted foil impressions, as described briefly overleaf.

> Scrub the foil into the stone until you have captured all the detail [using a nail brush as usual]. Spray the entire surface of the foil with . . . acrylic spray [paint] and allow it to dry. Next take a metallic paste and apply it carefully to the high points of the impression with your fingers. You may use the finger of an old cotton glove effectively for this. Be sure to apply the paste sparingly with short, wiping movements. When this is complete, simply remove the foil gently without bending it.

Any colour combinations are acceptable according to individual taste, but do use a daubing paste which will not react with the acrylic base. When the daubing is complete no part of the original foil remains and the combined colours on the relief surface do make a most attractive end product, although quite a long way removed from a conventional rubbing. Further ideas for mounting, displaying and using all types of rubbing are given in the next chapter.

5 Display and Further Ideas

As has been indicated throughout, the artistic production and presentation of rubbings is a particularly thorny subject. However, the sin of pleasure rubbing seems to apply only to those who rub and then display monumental brasses. Oddly enough, gravestone rubbers are apparently acceptable, so the 'crime' of brass rubbing cannot be considered one of spiritual omission. Perhaps because fewer people are interested in old graves, word of their activities has not yet gone abroad. One thing is clear however, no one can accuse you of lack of reverence if you have a wall covered in coal plate rubbings – although they may be moved to question your sanity!

Let us accept then that making rubbings is a pleasant hobby, that much can be gained from it if it is approached in the right frame of mind – and anyone reading this book must have a desire to know more about the subject – and that a little artistic licence is perfectly acceptable if it gives pleasure to the craftsman and those who look at the finished work, so long as it does not detract from the essential nature of the object rubbed. That being said, a few suggestions for working on rubbings and display ideas are given in the next few pages.

Finishing

All rubbings can be improved on. Many people take it as gospel that it is unacceptable to work on a rubbing when once it has been removed from the brass or stone. As has been shown in the last chapter this cannot apply to many rubbing methods, like making a positive rubbing, or with materials such as foil, which must be worked on afterwards to gain the desired effect. And, whilst a really good rubbing can look perfectly fine on its original paper – particularly the silver and gold figures on a black background – if hung between two simple rods, it does take practice to produce a rubbing worthy of this treatment.

For despite the upsurge of interest in brass rubbing and the help given by the centres, there are still many people who are too timid to press on the paper with the heelball as much as is needed to gain a good dense impression. They take up their grey rubbings and carry

35 Poor quality rubbing showing missing arm and line across brass. It can easily be darkened and the arm inserted as in illustration 5

them home where they hang dimly on walls like plaintive ghosts as in illustration 35. This incomplete lady, one of the wives of John Hauley of Dartmouth, can soon be spruced up with a little care and application. How to refurbish her missing arm has already been explained (page 17). Then, while she is positioned flat on a working surface, the overall colour can be darkened and the white lines brought out more if necessary, though it is remarkable how much whiter these look simply by making the black areas blacker.

Every book I have ever read on rubbings stresses how unwise it is to try to go over the impression with more wax after it has left the stone. Yet I have gone over the majority of my own rubbings in this way and, as far as I can tell, little irreparable damage has been done. In fact, in the eyes of most people who have seen them, they have been vastly improved. Of course, no one should attempt to darken a dress like that of the lace lady (page 21) with its complicated pattern, but wherever there are large dark areas these can be made darker. Obviously it is dangerous to work too close to the white lines but if you use an 'error card', as when doing the actual rubbing, little harm will be caused. For really fine lines it is possible to sharpen the heelball stick and use it like a blunt pencil. This is particularly effective for lettering on inscriptions or coal plates.

Another way of darkening poor rubbings is to paint over them with a thin brush and Indian ink (illustration 36). In the same way, the white lines can be cleaned up free from dark smudges with white ink, though a very delicate touch is needed here. If the rubbing is reasonably dark at the start it is sometimes necessary to neutralize the wax covering before applying the ink. However, all this seems a bit of a waste of time when the rubbing has been deliberately taken with wax in the first place. Also, the ink produces a matt black surface and is not as impressive as the shine which can be given to heelball.

Where known, the original colours can be put back on parts of rubbings like the shields of armed figures, the heraldic tabards worn by some ladies and the small representations of arms which were essential to many brasses. Simply trace over the part to be coloured on a separate sheet, then paint in the appropriate shades and stick onto the rubbing. After my own experience with the blue-and-gold shield of Sir John D'Aubernoun (page 14) I am averse to this kind of finishing as the colours should really be seen in conjunction with the

36 This unusual design coal plate has been finished by inking in the dark lines and the lettering, then mounted on coloured card

subtle bronze brass rather than the harder black of the rubbing, yet can appreciate that some people like the added touch of authenticity with such colouring gives.

Mounting

Brass rubbing centres sell graded sets of black plastic strips with which to hang rubbings and hold them straight. These strips, also available in white from most stores selling posters and prints, do ensure that the rubbing hangs well (they are used to hold the coal plate rubbing of the dog and pot, page 85) but are very tight-fitting and can tear thin paper if care is not taken when putting them on.

This is just one of the many reasons why it is a good idea to give rubbings a more permanent backing than the paper on which they are rubbed. However, because all paper stretches when rubbed, it is extremely difficult to stick a rubbing to a solid background such as board without its wrinkling horribly. I nearly always cut out my rubbings – the dog and the pot design, being on a hand-made paper is an exception as it did not stretch, and as the background colour was so suitable I simply stuck the whole sheet on a firm card – which minimizes the wrinkles but still leaves room for a little distortion.

I therefore prefer to mount the rubbings on material rather than board as the softness of a linen or silky fabric will yield with the slightly stretched paper of the rubbing. If allowed to hang free, not fixed tight to the wall, the hanging will have a slight undulating movement instead of showing definite ripples across the actual rubbing. As material is usually bought in metres, unless you are lucky enough to pick up a remnant like the 'flawed' piece of brown roller blind on which young Elizabeth Culpeper is mounted (cover), it will have to be cut carefully to the size of the rubbing, leaving a few inches between top and bottom and at each side, then sewn. Machine stitching is simple and looks quite effective – so long as the stitches are straight. For more delicate rubbings such as the Lace Lady, I prefer to catch the turned-back hems at the back of the rubbing so that the stitches do not show.

Leave enough material at both ends so that it can be turned over an inch or so, before being sewn, leaving the sides open so that some form of rod can be inserted at top and bottom to hold the rubbing firm. Bamboo canes of varying thickness as used in the garden are inexpensive and look attractive with most materials. They can be split quite easily with a handsaw to the required length. Cut them a few inches longer than the width of the mounted rubbing so that the top cane can have hanging cord tied round each end and the bottom will balance with it.

Hessian also makes a good tough backing for rubbings such as coal plates and can be bought in many colours. My sister mounted a positive and negative rubbing of the same figure on the stiff hessian used for wall covering (illustration 37). These look most impressive but, as they are difficult to roll, cannot be moved around easily. By contrast, a rubbing which was mounted on a rush mat – one with a coarse grain like a beach mat – was rolled up for a journey and then forgotten until several months later when it emerged virtually as good as new.

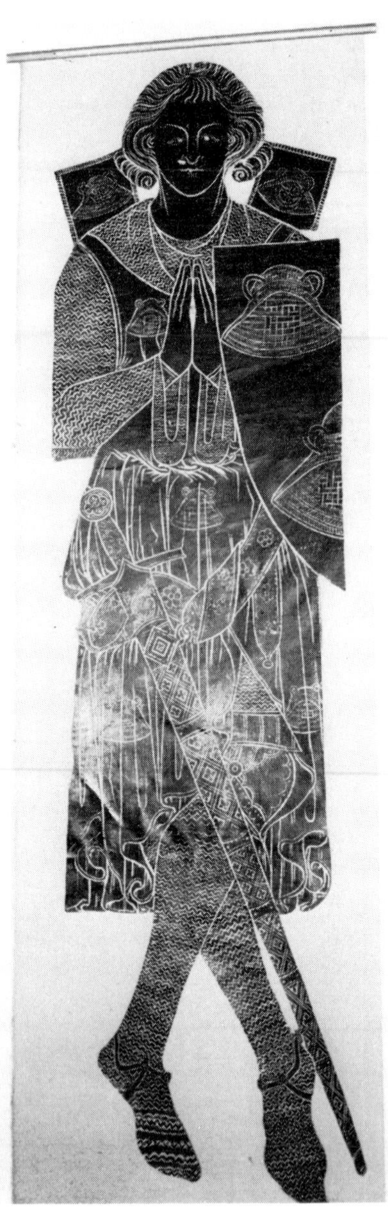

37 Hessian-backed rubbing of the brass to Sir Robert de Septvans (1306), Chartham, Kent. The finely engraved brass showing complete mail armour is unusual for the curly hair. Note the difficulty of photographing both brasses and rubbings as the flash often catches the bronze or wax

My major error with early rubbings was caused not by stretched paper nor unsuitable backings but by a clumsy method of sticking the rubbing to the chosen backing material. Using any old branded glue I pasted it liberally on the figure, stuck down something as large as a six-foot knight in one swift movement, put heavy books on top and waited a day or so for a good adhesion. This really is the way to ensure wrinkles as it is well nigh impossible to position a large figure in one movement without a lot of rippling and, once stuck so firmly in place, the paper cannot be moved without tearing.

Now I would not be without a bonded spray adhesive which becomes tacky within seconds of being applied to one surface only and can be repositioned easily if the rubbing is misplaced in any way. This spray also does not stain and needs no great weight to ensure a firm bond. It also claims to retain its adhesive qualities for years.

A large can of adhesive spray will go a long way but it *is* very expensive. An alternative which can be recommended is a clear wallpaper paste like 'Polycell' which also gives a tight bond and can be stored in a glass jar if too much has been made up at once. Glue under the brand name 'Cow Gum' can be peeled off if there is any difficulty in the mounting, and flour-and-water paste makes a useful standby, although it should be applied sparingly if it is not to soak through.

One truly wrinkle-free mounting technique is to 'press' the rubbing between glass or clear acetate (available at stationers supplying detail paper) and a backing board. By simply taping the top of the rubbing to the backing the rest can hang free and will never be subject to those disfiguring ripples caused by actually gluing it to an inflexible backing. After carefully cutting round the rubbing, either tape it lightly direct to the backing if you are using wood with an attractive grain, or put a piece of plain paper, of whatever colour you wish, behind it to hide the hardboard or whatever. Then roll out the acetate over the whole board and again tape it securely out of sight. Although unsightly at the back, this looks perfectly good from the front as it is, and can be hung without any further refinements. Glass must have a frame however. As these are expensive or time-consuming to construct, and as a large, framed glass-mounted rubbing is very heavy, I would not recommend this method except perhaps for exhibition purposes.

Dabbings can be mounted exactly as rubbings, only here I first attach them to a sheet of textured paper or card to give the flimsy tissue more 'body'. Use the spray adhesive which is particularly good for fine papers. Foil rubbings should preferably not be covered as it is all too easy to press out their indentation. They are best mounted on a fairly heavy board and hung as a picture but can be heavy and difficult to move.

Display

Rubbings will be used according to personal tastes but, in the same way in which there is little point in hanging a poor rubbing, so an ill-positioned rubbing is not doing justice to its subject or the craft which has produced it. Do not simply use rubbings, as one person put it, 'to fill up a few bare walls'. Make them focal points, either hanging alone, possibly on a light wall for emphasis by contrast or, spot-lit on a dark wall. If there is space, arrange them in an appealing group. Put them where they can be looked at constantly and will be a talking point. Someone I know has large military figures flanking the chimney breast in the dining room. Someone else has a frieze of ladies' head-dresses from brasses all round the top of her daughter's bedroom. I use two large brass rubbings to take away the awful emptiness of gaping stairwells punctured by hideous black tubes which are a modern apology for bannisters. And one eligible bachelor even has rubbings on his bed head!

It is not silly or vain to match your rubbings to your decor. A purple-coloured lady on a white background will not look good on an orange wall. Similarly a hearty coal plate rubbing will all too obviously be out of place in a room with pastel or even chintz furnishings. Colour schemes change, of course, which is why it is perhaps wise to stick to neutral, or at least favourite shades for backings, if you want to keep the rubbings on display for a long time.

If you have lots of rubbings don't give them all away. Rubbings do make attractive gifts, though they are not always gratefully received; one quite level-headed friend said he could not bear to keep looking into the unseeing eyes of the brass rubbing which I had so proudly given him. No, change the rubbings around as frequently as possible. You will gain great pleasure from seeing old favourites after the initial appeal of a new rubbing has worn off.

38 The dog with its head in a pot coal plate rubbing makes a wall hanging with a difference

This brings up the difficult question of storage. Paper will eventually grow brittle with age, even when mounted on fabric. It will also fade, as will the fabric if not hidden from the light. Huge portfolios of rubbings may look impressive but are difficult to pack away in modern houses with little storage space. They are also a dangerous way of keeping fabric-backed rubbings as the material only needs to become accidentally folded over, then the leaves pressed together for a long period and the rubbing will crease badly. It is preferable to roll rubbings lightly and learn to accept the occasional wrinkle as inevitable. At least a fabric backing can be ironed and much of the damage undone. Foil rubbings will most likely be on hardboard and, as such, can only be lain face upwards in attics, on top of wardrobes, under beds and in all the other usual storage places for flat items.

Finally, if you are in danger of being turned out of the house by an invasion of rubbings, then don't be greedy but ask if friends and neighbours might like one, on loan as it were. Local libraries are often only too pleased to add something worthwhile to their stock, and schools use rubbings as teaching aids, as well as starting children off on this hobby.

Further Ideas

Brass rubbings as wall hangings, yes; brass rubbings on waste-paper baskets, no. This is the view expressed by one authority on brasses, again based on the belief that whilst a hanging can be suitably serious and in keeping with a memorial figure, it is poor taste to decorate utility objects with such rubbings. I agree up to a point. Much of the commercial exploitation of brass rubbings has been in the miniaturizing of the subjects and putting them on anything from the afore-mentioned waste bins to tea towels. And, whilst there can be nothing wrong in a mini-rubbing on a book mark or a greetings card, I do object to the cheapening of these fine brasses by their garish representations on tin trays and frosted drinking glasses.

However, it seems to me that there is a great difference between something made by hand, in the home for personal satisfaction, and a mass-produced item. Thus, while always bearing in mind what brasses stand for, we surely cannot take objection to small rubbings used to enhance a simple wicker or straw basket even if waste is deposited there. Similarly, using a rubbing of a carved top of a gravestone to form an archway over a door is hardly irreverent, and incorporating a telling memorial inscription into a tray would seem a nice idea.

This may be splitting hairs but, while actively disliking those sets of place mats bearing representations of brass rubbings, I gain great pleasure from my own rubbings of the Signs of the Four Evangelists captured on cork as place mats. The symbols: the eagle, St John; the winged ox, St Luke; a winged lion, St Mark, and an angel with a scroll, St Matthew, were frequently found at the four corners of the rectangular border containing an inscription which surrounded many fifteenth-century brasses. The ones on my mats come from a facsimile brass, the original being in the Rijksmuseum, Amsterdam. The main part of the brass to Gijsbert Willemszoen de Raet, 1511, is a trefoil plate with an angel holding two shields. It is full of marvellous detail, and I cannot yet decide quite how it should be mounted.

The evangelical symbols were rubbed with a bronze heelball on white detail paper, then cut out. Two thin cork carpet tiles were stuck together to form the mats, and cut carefully in circles slightly larger than the actual symbols. These were then stuck lightly to the

39 Lampshade displaying rubbings of a woolmark (shown here), a nativity scene and an evangelical symbol

cork with adhesive spray and given about four coats of clear, heat-resistant polyurethane varnish. They are quite crude looking but that is not displeasing. On reflection I would have preferred to rub the signs with a darker wax, certainly not a metallic one, which would have stood out more against the warm brown of the cork instead of fading into the background as these tend to.

There seems no need either to apologize for the child's bedside lamp which uses brass rubbings for decoration. Indeed, this may be a most fitting home for the rubbings as the lamp brings light and comfort while, at the same time, providing a source of learning. Only small rubbings can be used for such a project, and again it is difficult to find suitable ones. The three used on this lamp (illustration 39) are of just the right size and subject matter. The lamb is, appropriately enough, a woolmark from the brass of Thomas Busshe, 1526, a wool merchant of Northleach, Gloucester. There is also an exquisite nativity scene and a winged eagle, the symbol for St John. They were rubbed in different colours, the lamb in bronze, the nativity in black and the eagle in green. Again, a lighter colour would have been more in keeping with the scene in the stable but might not have been as effective on the lamp when lit.

The original plan was to use a plain parchment shade and simply stick the rubbings, facing outwards, inside the shade so that they sprang into life when the light was used. In the event, the only shade available with sufficient see-through quality did lend itself to this treatment but the figures looked very dull when the bulb was not glowing through. As the lamp will spend the majority of its days unlit, it seemed preferable to stick the rubbings at intervals round the outside of the shade. This proved most effective and the lamp could well have remained like this. To combat dust and sticky fingers, however, I thought it best to cover the shade with a sheet of self-adhesive transparent plastic, the type used for covering book jackets which is obtainable from most large stationers.

These are but two examples of the different ways in which all kinds of rubbings can be used. The more you experiment, the more ideas will spring to mind bringing greater satisfaction. Why not make a rubbing collage by assembling such diverse objects as curved string, some matches, hair grips, a comb, a piece of lace or anything of interesting shape and texture? It's best to glue the objects to a piece

40 Oriental stone rubbing mounted on an old prie-dieu and used to display houseplants

of card before rubbing so that they don't move under the paper and spoil the effect. Form them into a scene or an abstract pattern then employ different techniques and colours to achieve a really striking picture.

It's easy to make your own gift wrap which is inexpensive and adds a personal touch. Dabbing on coloured tissue paper is particularly effective with a pattern of leaves or a piece of tree bark repeated over and over. Remember to take off brittle stems on dried leaves or tough stalks on pressed flower heads so as not to tear the paper.

A pretty design rubbed or dabbed on a coloured background can be covered with clear plastic to make a useful door plate to counteract sticky or dirty fingers. It can be put under glass to form the centrepoint of a wooden tray. It can be mounted on a piece of thin card to make a book mark or even stuck down on a fly leaf as one of the old-fashioned name book plates which are becoming popular again. Make your own greetings cards from rubbings. Incorporate them in wallpaper, on writing paper, in book bindings. The opportunities for creative enjoyment with rubbings is virtually endless.

Further Reading

Books and pamphlets on monuments, and especially on brasses and brass rubbing, abound. They range from hardback volumes available through bookshops such as a reprint of 'the finest nineteenth century book on the subject' containing coloured engravings, J. G. and L. A. R. Waller's *A Series of Monumental Brasses from the Thirteenth to the Sixteenth Centuries*, to leaflets obtainable from specific brass rubbing centres, like *Brass Rubbing at Westminster Abbey*, an eight-page illustrated introduction. There are also many titles which cover the country area by area, such as the Studio 69 series of county guides. Phillips & Page (see Appendix A) have a comprehensive stock of such books and a complete list, with prices, can be obtained from their mail order division at 40, Elm Hill, Norwich NR3 1HG.

Gravestones too are covered in some detail in many specialist publications, although usually taking second place behind stone tombs and effigies sculptured in the round. The general reader will probably gain most from leaflets produced by the churches themselves, or from a good topographical series such as the forty-two volumes of Arthur Mee's *The King's England.*

Street furniture is not so well represented, so the reader seeking more detail on coal plates, pillar boxes and other forms of public utilities may be best advised to consult a library to gain access to old records or out of print volumes.

Titles given below are of those books which I personally have read and found most useful. Brief notes summarize their main points of interest.

Bertram, Jerome. *Brasses and Brass Rubbing in England*, David & Charles, 1971 (Good, comprehensive text, poor illustrations)

Cook, Malcolm. *Discovering Brasses and Brass Rubbing*, Shire, 1971 (Usual detailed coverage from this pocket paperback series)

Farrugia, Jean Young. *The Letter Box, A History of Post Office Pillar and Wall Boxes*, Centaur Press, 1969 (Standard, containing countrywide list of where to see old boxes, with good line drawings for identification)

Franklyn, Julian. *Brasses*, Arco, 1964 (Purist, detailed, special section on how to read inscriptions)

Mann, James. *Monumental Brasses*, King Penguin, 1957 (Authoritative coverage of armour and costume)

McGeer, William. *Reproducing Relief Surfaces*, 1972 (Sub-title, *A Complete Handbook of Rubbing, Dabbing, Casting and Daubing* says it all. Excellent American ingenuity for all ages)

Morris, Sally. *Brass Rubbing in Devon Churches*, 1967 (Idiosyncratic ramble through countryside with good directions, descriptions)

Norris, Malcolm. *Brass Rubbing*, Studio Vista, 1965/Pan, 1977 (Heavily illustrated, details of European brasses)

Norris M. and Kellett, M. *Your Book of Brasses*, Faber, 1974 (Good, popular introduction, section on photographing brasses)

Page-Phillips, John. *Macklin's Monumental Brasses*, Allen and Unwin, 1973 (Revamp of the classic manual with good county lists of brasses)

Smith, Edwin. Cook, Olive and Hutton, Graham. *English Parish Churches*, Thames & Hudson, 1976 (The late Edwin Smith's 214 remarkable photographs with explanatory text)

Taylor, Dr Shephard T. (under pen name of 'Sketches by Aesculapius Junior'). *Opercula (London Coal Plates)*, reprinted from the *Ironmonger*, 1929 (150 line drawings of London plates existing in 1863)

Warren, Geoffrey. *Vanishing Street Furniture*, David and Charles, 1978 (Detailed, illustrated, from bollards to water closets)

Years of Reflection 1783–1953, The Story of Haywards of the Borough (Private publishing of fascinating company history of iron founders)

Appendix A
Useful Addresses

The Monumental Brass Society, c/o Society of Antiquaries, Burlington House, London W1 (welcomes members with a genuine interest in the preservation of brasses and encourages original research)

The Friends of the Friendless Churches, c/o the Hon. Director, 12 Edwardes Square, London W8 6HG (rescues derelict churches and preserves condemned ones)

Phillips & Page, 50 Kensington Church Street, London W8 (specialize in rubbing equipment and carry a comprehensive range of books. Sell finished rubbings and also hand-made brass and stone facsimiles)

Brass Rubbing Supplies, 48a Ashcroft Rd, Cirencester, Glos. (part of Brass Rubbing Centres Ltd which has four permanent centres at Bristol, Oxford, York and Stratford, as well as seasonal exhibitions through the country – see Appendix C. Send stamped addressed envelope for mail order price list of materials)

Falkiner Fine Paper Ltd, 4 Mart Street, London WC2 (extensive range of handmade papers suitable for all types of rubbing, but not cheap)

Appendix B
Where to See Rubbings

In a country so rich in brasses – and once considerably richer – many county town museums and other institutions have been able to establish valuable collections of rubbings. As the majority of these are not on permanent display, it is best to consult a local library or museum to find out what is available in any particular area. There are, however, several outstanding collections of brasses and other objects discussed in this book which genuine enthusiasts should attempt to see.

Society of Antiquaries, Burlington House, London W1 (the most complete collection of brass rubbings, arranged by county)

Victoria and Albert Museum, Exhibition Road, London SW7 (large collection arranged by area in the Print Room. *Catalogue of Rubbings of Brasses and Incised Slabs* on sale. Collection of heraldic stone rubbings. Details of coal plates)

British Museum, Bloomsbury, London WC1 (several collections including the famous eighteenth-century work of Ord and Cullum, page 70)

The Museum of London, Barbican, London EC1 (large collection of coal plate rubbings, not permanently on view)

Chartered Insurance Institute, 20 Aldermanbury, London EC2 (World's largest collection of British fire marks. Also museum with early examples of fire-fighting equipment)

Ashmolean Museum, Oxford (fine collection, arranged by area. *Notes on Brass Rubbing* available)

Museum of Archaeology and Ethnology, Cambridge (comprehensive collection of good rubbings)

National Postal Museum, King Edward Street, London EC1 (most extensive collection of postage stamps in world. Information on all Post Office matters, including pillar boxes)

Appendix C
Brass Rubbing Centres

Recent and continuing interest in rubbing is a source of concern to many who do not wish to see the ancient brasses gradually eroded. Many churches no longer allow rubbing, while several important brasses are now under glass. In order to preserve existing brasses yet still encourage rubbing, centres have been established round the country containing reproduction brasses which can be rubbed for realistic sums. Centres are in:

Bath

The Friends Meeting House, York Street (off Abbey Churchyard)
Free admission. Materials for sale. Instruction given.

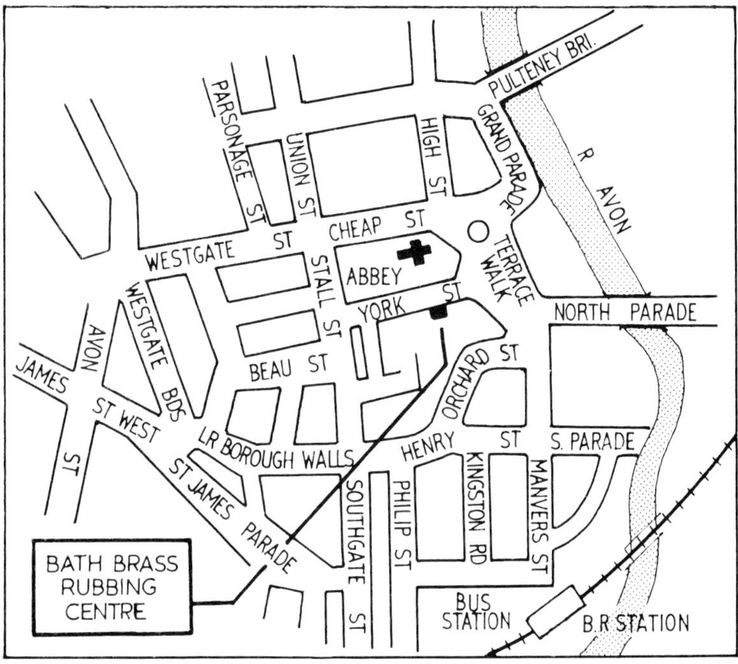

Bath. The Friends' Meeting House, York Street

Open throughout summer from 1 Jun, Mon–Sat, 10 am–5.30 pm, Sun 1 pm–5.30 pm. Tel: Bristol (0272) 423397.

Bristol

St Nicholas Church and City Museum, Baldwin Street. Open all year, 10 am–5 pm, daily except Sun.

Cambridge

Wesley Church Library, King Street
Free admission. Materials and finished rubbings on sale. Coffee and biscuits. Group bookings taken.
Open all year, Tues, Wed, Thurs, Sat 10 am–5 pm and every day except Sunday throughout Jul and Aug. Tel: Cambridge 61318.

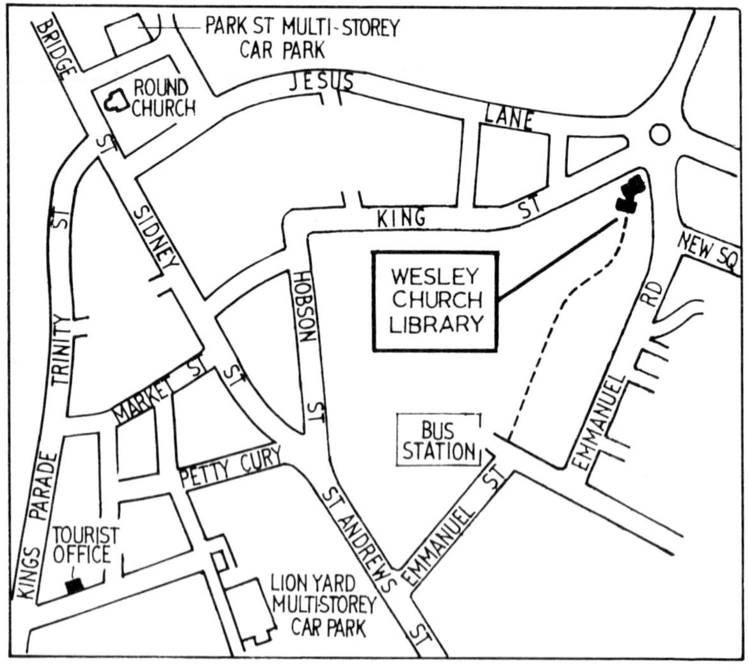

Cambridge. The Library, Wesley Church, King Street

Canterbury

Sidney Cooper Building, St Peter's Street, nr Westgate
Free admission. Materials provided.
Open Mon–Sat, 10 am–6 pm, Sun 12 pm–6 pm

The Old Weavers, Kings Bridge.
Open every day 9 Apr–Oct.

Chichester

The Cloisters, Chichester Cathedral
Open mid-Jun–mid-Sept, 10 am–5 pm

Coventry

The Cathedral, Wyley Chapel
Open Jul–Oct, Mon–Sat, 10.30 am–5 pm, Sun 3 pm–6 pm

Dodington

Dodington House, Glos (junction 18 on M4)
Open Easter and Jun–mid-Sept, 12 noon–6 pm daily.

Edinburgh

Canongate Tolbooth, Royal Mile
Open Apr–Oct, Mon–Sat, 10 am–6 pm

St John's Church, Princes' Street.
Free admission. Instruction and materials available.
Open throughout summer from 1 Jun, Mon–Sat, 10 am–6 pm,
Sun 1 pm–5 pm

Glastonbury

St John's Church, High Street
Free admission. Instruction and materials available.
Open throughout summer from 15 Jul–Sep, Mon–Sat,
10 am–5 pm, Sun 1 pm–5pm

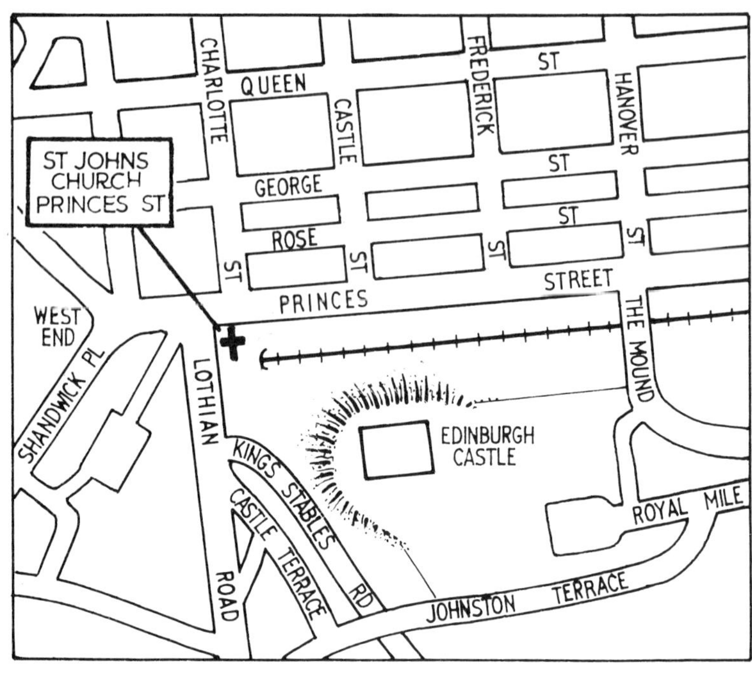

Edinburgh. St John's Church, Princes Street

Gloucester

The Cathedral
Open Jul–Sep, Mon–Sat 10 am–5 pm

London

All Hallow's Church, Byward Street, EC3 (next to Tower of London)
Open Mon–Sat 10.30 am–6 pm, Sun 12.30 pm–6 pm

Greenwich Brass Rubbing Centre, 15 Nelson Road, SE10

St George's Church, Aubrey Walk, off Campden Hill, W8
Free admission. Materials and books on sale. 60 brasses.
Light refreshments.
Open Mon, Tues, Thurs, Sat 10 am–5 pm, Fri 2 pm–9 pm

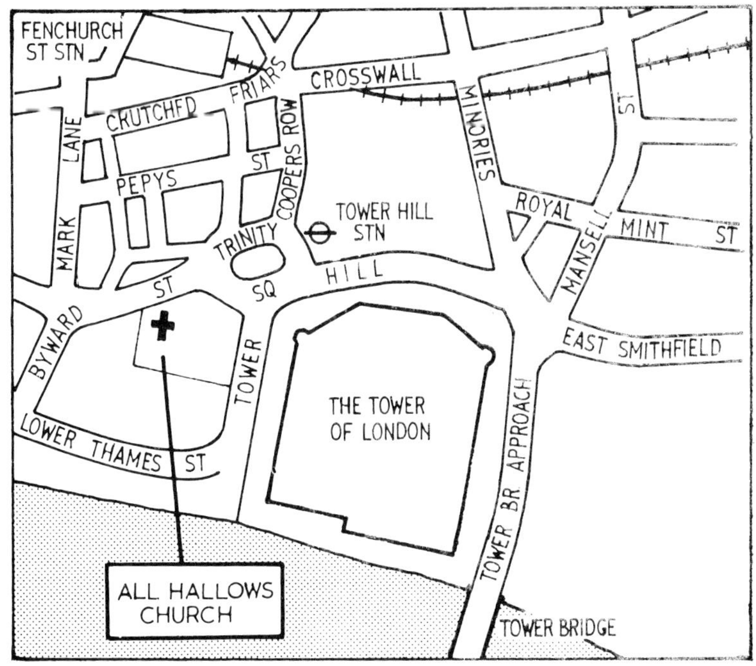

London. All Hallows Church, beside the Tower of London, Byward Street, EC3

St James's Church, Piccadilly, W1
Free admission. Materials and instruction available. Own booklet, *Brasses Historical Notes* by Tim Tiley, co-owner.
Open throughout year, Mon–Sat 10 am–6 pm, Sun 12 pm–6 pm

Westminster Abbey
Cloisters, Mon–Sat 10 am–5.30 pm
St Margaret's Church, Mon–Sat 9.30 am–6 pm

Marlborough

St Peter's Church
Open Jul–Sept, 10 am–6 pm daily.

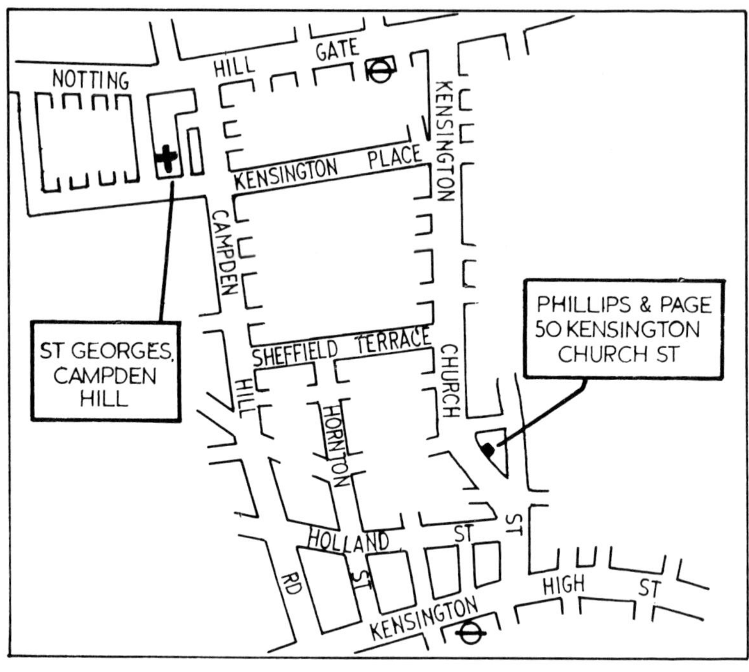

London. Phillips and Page, 50 Kensington Church Street, W8, and St George's, Aubrey Walk

Newcastle–upon–Tyne

Laing Art Gallery
Open mid-Jul–mid-Sept, Tues–Thurs 10 am–5.30 pm, Sun 2.30 pm–5.30 pm

Nottingham

St Mary's Church, High Pavement, The Lacemarket
Open mid-Jul–mid-Sept, Mon–Sat, 10.30 am–6 pm, Sun 2 pm–6 pm

Oxford

University Church of St Mary the Virgin, High St
Open throughout the year, 10 am–6 pm, daily

The Museum of Oxford, St Aldates
Open mid-Jul–beg Sept, Tues–Sat, 10 am–5 pm

Winchester

The Museum, nr Cathedral
Open 10 am–5 pm (small collection).

Windsor

St John the Baptist, High Street (next to the Guildhall)
Open every day from 10 am–4 pm. Materials, etc provided.

Woodstock

Oxford County Museum
Open mid-Jul–beg Sept, Mon–Fri, 10 am–5 pm, Sat till 6 pm, Sun 2 pm–6 pm

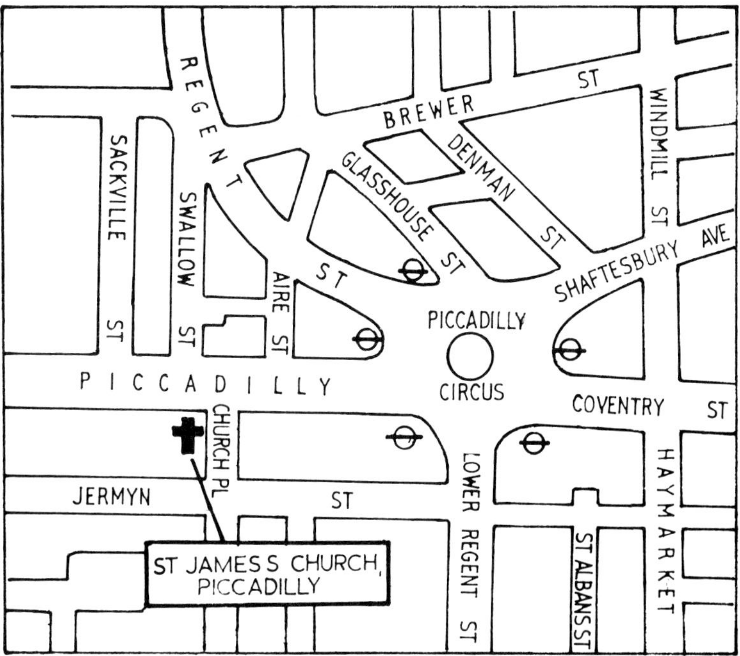

London. St James's Church, Piccadilly, W1

United States

English Brass Rubbing Centre, 1142 W Washington Blvd, Venice 90291, California 396-4442
33 facsimiles. Free classes. Brass and stone rubbings from Europe.
Open every day except Mon, 10 am–5 pm

Robbie's Brass Rubbing Centre, 609 Westbury Sq, Houston, Texas
European facsimiles.

Appendix D
Top 30 Churches with Brasses

The rich heritage of England's 10,000 brasses must make any attempt to list the 'best' appear somewhat unnecessary. Such a list must also be open to question in that conflicting opinions may exist among experts as to dating, artistry, relevance and so on. Yet it can be argued that amidst such a vast wealth of brasses, some help in pinpointing the most important is performing a real service. And consultation of several authorities does reveal a common concensus of these genuinely outstanding remaining brasses. Their views, backed up wherever possible by personal knowledge, has produced the following guide. It should be of use to overseas visitors with little time to spare by enabling them to plan itineraries round specific brasses. It will also provide an at-a-glance reference for enthusiasts who might well know about, say the Trumpington brass in Cambridgeshire, but not the one at Westley Waterless.

The list is compiled alphabetically by county. Except where specifically noted – as with an Abbey or a town with several ancient churches – the church will always be the local parish church.

Brass rubbing is not permitted at all the following churches. It is not allowed, for instance, at Cobham, Kent where the finest selection of brasses in the country are to be found.

How to Use the Guide

Key:

 armed figure

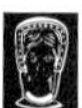 female

 civilian

 child

 ecclesiastical

The categories chosen represent the most common figures on brasses. Where these require further explanation, the following abbreviations are used:

Ab, Abbot; ac, Academic; A/B, Archbishop; B, Bishop; F, Flemish; h, heart; j, judge; m, monk; p, palimpsest; s, shroud; SS, saints; symb., symbolic; X, cross

The child symbol stands for an individual brass to a child and does not include the many children who appear with their parents.

Figures are given in chronological order.

Identical dates on the same line but under separate categories, eg

1502 1502

normally indicate two figures on the same brass and, as in the above case, usually husband and wife.

Numbers in parenthesis by a date indicate the total number of figures in that category, eg 1442(2) means that two women are on that brass.

Location					
BUCKINGHAMSHIRE					
Thornton	1472	1472(3)			
		1557			
CAMBRIDGESHIRE					
Balsham					1401(s)
					1462(s)
	c1480				
Trumpington	1289				
Westley Waterless	1325	1325			
ESSEX					
Little Easton					c1420
	1483	1483			
Pebmarsh	1323				
GLOUCESTERSHIRE					
Deerhurst		1400	1400(j)		1400(s)
		c1520			
		1525			
Chipping Camden		1401	1401		
		1450	1450		
		1467	1467		
		1484(3)	1484		
Cirencester	1438				
		1440	1440		
		1442(4)	1442		
					c1475(symb.)
	1462	1462(2)			
		1470			
					1478
					c1480
		c1480	c1480		
		1497(2)			
			c1500		
		c1500	c1500		
		c1530(2)			
			1587		
		1626	1626		
HAMPSHIRE					
Thruxton	1425				
HEREFORDSHIRE					
Hereford Cathedral					1282(s)
					1360(B)
					1386(X)
			1394		
	1435	1435			
					1476(SS)
			1480		
	c1480				
	1514	1514(2)			
					c1520
					1524(SS)
					1529(SS)

Location					
HERTFORDSHIRE					
St Albans Abbey					c1375(Ab & SS, F)
		1411	1411		
					c1450(m)
					c1460(m)
	1468	1468			
			1519		
					1521(m)
KENT					
Chartham	1306				
					1416
					1454
					1508
		1530			
Cobham		1320			
	1354				
	c1356				
	1367				
		1375			
		1380			
		1395			
					1402
	1402				
	1405				
	1407				
					1418
		1433			
					c1450
					1498
		1506			
	1529	1529			
Hever		1419(symb.)			
	1538		1585		
LINCOLNSHIRE					
Linwood		1419	1419		
			1421		
Tattershall			1411		
					1456
					1470(SS)
		1470			1470(SS)
		1475			1475(SS)
					1510(SS)
					1519
LONDON					
Enfield		c1470			
		1592	1592		
Westminster Abbey					1395(B & SS)
					1397(A/B)
		1399			
	1438				

Location					
LONDON	1483				
Westminster Abbey					1498(A/B)
contd	1505				
					1561
NORFOLK					
Elsing	1347				1347(SS)
Felbrigg		c1380			
	1416	1416			
		c1480			
	c1608				
		1608			
King's Lynn					
St Margaret		1349	1349(symb./F)		
		1364(2)	1364(symb./F)		
NORTHAMPTONSHIRE					
Higham Ferrers					1337(SS)
					1400(SS)
		1425	1425		
		c1435			
					1498
					c1500(h)
		1504	1504		
			1518		
					1523
			c1540(2)		
NOTTINGHAMSHIRE					
Newark			1361(F)		1361(SS)
			c1540		
			1557		
OXFORDSHIRE					
Childrey	1444	1444(2)			1477(s symb.)
					c1480
		c1480	c1480		
	1514(symb.)	1514			
					1516(s)
		c1520	c1520		
			1529(ac)		
SURREY					
Stoke d'Abernon	1277				
	1327				
		1464			
				1516	
		1592	1592		
SUSSEX (WEST)					
Trotton		c1310			
	1419	1419			

Location					
WARWICKSHIRE					
Warwick, St Mary	1406	1406 1573	 1573		
WILTSHIRE					
Salisbury Cathedral					1375(B in castle) 1578(B)
YORKSHIRE (NORTH)					
Wensley					1375(F)

Appendix E
Outstanding Brasses – Where to Find Them

The following list shows the major 250 locations of brasses to be found nationwide. It is given alphabetically, by county and uses the 'new' county names. Bear this in mind when using the list with an old map, as some counties such as Rutland have, of course, disappeared altogether, while towns and villages have crossed over borders into different counties – Wantage is now in Oxfordshire, not Berkshire – and strange names such as Humberside and Avon are not readily assimilated.

As usual, the parish church is the main home of brasses. However, some of the brasses listed are to be found in university colleges, and one Flemish brass from the now demolished church of St Mary, Ipswich, is in that town's Christchurch Mansion. Some of these brasses have been restored and others have been moved to new homes, such as those now in St Mary Redcliffe, Bristol, which come from bombed churches in the city.

Permission must always be obtained before rubbing, though again not all these brasses can be rubbed. The fine series at Harrow, for example, are not available for rubbing and the 1320 cross at Chinnor, Oxford, is also 'out of bounds'. Special dispensation has to be obtained to rub in St George's Chapel, Windsor.

Less important brasses throughout the country are also protected by glass and so are not able to be rubbed. But this list indicates only truly outstanding brasses. Anyone seeking a comprehensive guide to all brasses of whatever quality must consult Mill Stephenson's 1926 *List of Monumental Brasses in the British Isles*, reprinted with Appendix by the Monumental Brass Society.

AVON

Dyrham; Bristol St Mary Redcliffe; Winterbourne

BEDFORDSHIRE
Apsley Guise; Bromham; Cardington; Cople; Elstow; Eyworth; Marston Mortaine; Shillington; Wymington

BERKSHIRE
Bray; Eton College Chapel; Shottesbrook; Windsor St George's Chapel

BUCKINGHAMSHIRE
Chenies; Denham; Drayton Beauchamp; Edlesborough; Middle Claydon; Pitstone; Stoke Poges; Taplow; Thornton; Twyford; Upper Winchendon; Waddesdon

CAMBRIDGESHIRE
Balsham; Burwell; Cambridge King's College, St John's College, Trinity Hall; Diddington; Ely Cathedral; Fulbourne; Hildersham; Ilesham; Little Shelford; Sawtry; Trumpington; Westley Waterless

CHESHIRE
Macclesfield; Wilmslow; Winwick

CORNWALL
East Antony; Lanteglos; St Mellion

CUMBRIA
Carlisle; Edenhall

DERBYSHIRE
Ashbourne; Morley; Mugginton; Tideswell

DEVON
Dartmouth St Saviour; Stoke Fleming

DORSET
Thornecombe

DURHAM
Sedgefield

ESSEX

Aveley; Bowers Gifford; Chigwell; Chrishall; Great Bromley; Ingrave; Little Easton; Little Horkesley; Pebmarsh; Wimbish; Wivenhoe

GLOUCESTERSHIRE

Chipping Camden; Deerhurst; Cirencester; Gloucester, St Mary de Crypt; Northleach; Wootton-under-Edge; Wormington

GREATER LONDON

All Hallows Barking, EC3; Beddington, Croydon; East Wickham, Greenwich; Enfield; Fulham; Harrow; Hillingdon; Westminster Abbey

HAMPSHIRE AND ISLE OF WIGHT

Crondall; Havant; King's Somborne; Ringwood; Stoke Charity; Thruxton; Winchester, St Cross Isle of Wight: Freshwater

HEREFORDSHIRE

Clehonger; Hereford Cathedral

HERTFORDSHIRE

Aldbury; Berkhamsted; Broxbourne; Digswell; Hemel Hempstead; Hunsdon; Knebworth; North Mimms; St Albans, Abbey and St Michael; Sawbridgeworth; Standon; Watford; Watton-at-Stone

HUMBERSIDE

Barton, St Mary; Brandsburton; Cottingham; Harpham

KENT

Addington; Ashford; Bobbing; Chartham; Cobham; Dartford; East Sutton; Faversham; Graveney; Herne; Hever; Horsmonden; Kemsing; Lydd; Mereworth; Minster; Northfleet; Otterden; Saltwood; Seal; Stone; Ulcombe; Upper Hardres; Woodchurch

LEICESTERSHIRE

Bottesford; Castle Donington; Little Casterton

LINCOLNSHIRE

Boston, St Botolph; Broughton; Buslingthorpe; Croft; Gedney; Grainthorpe; Gunby; Irnham; Laughton; Linwood; Spilsby; Stamford, All Saints; Tattershall

NORFOLK

Blickling; Burnham Thorpe; Elsing; Erpingham; Felbrigg; Fransham; Gorleston; Hunstanton; Ketteringham; King's Lynn, St Margaret; Methwold; Narborough; Norwich, St George's Colegate, St John Maddermarket, St Lawrence; Reepham; Rougham; Shernbourne; Southacre; Upwell

NORTHAMPTONSHIRE

Ashby St Legers; Brampton; Castle Ashby; Charwelton; Cotterstock; Easton Heston; Greens Norton; Higham Ferrers; Lowick; Nether Heyford; Newton; Rothwell

NOTTINGHAMSHIRE

East Markham; Newark; Strelley

OXFORDSHIRE

Blewbury; Brightwell Baldwin; Cassington; Checkendon; Childrey; Chinnor; Ewelme; Great Tew; Hanney; Mapledurham; Oxford, Merton College, New College; Rotherfield; Sparsholt; Thame; Wantage

SHROPSHIRE

Acton Burnell; Tong

SOMERSET

Ilminster; South Petherton

STAFFORDSHIRE

Audley; Clifton Campville; Norbury; Okeover

SUFFOLK

Acton; Burgate; Ipswich Christchurch Mansion; Playford; Rougham; Stoke-by-Nayland

SURREY
East Horsley; Lingfield; Stoke d'Abernon

SUSSEX
East: Buxted; Etchingham; Fletching; Herstmonceux; Trotton; Warbleton

West: Ardingly; Arundel; Broadwater; Clapham; Cowfold; Horley; West Grinstead; Wiston

TYNE-AND-WEAR
Newcastle, All Saints

WARWICKSHIRE
Baginton; Merevale; Warwick, St Mary; Wixford

WILTSHIRE
Cliffe Pypard; Dauntsey; Draycot Cerne; Mere; Salisbury Cathedral

WORCESTERSHIRE
Fladbury; Kidderminster; Strensham

YORKSHIRE
North: Aldbrough; Topcliffe; Wensley; York Minster

Appendix F
London Brasses, North and South of the Thames

A separate appendix devoted to London churches alone was deemed to be of use in that it represents a truly amazing concentration of brasses of all types in any one area. Also, the capital is obviously an area which will be visited more frequently by brass enthusiasts, particularly those from overseas, than a more far-flung country area.

Churches are given alphabetically under location and are named to prevent time-wasting in a large suburb with two or more churches, City churches being presented under 'C' in the North of the Thames section.

How to Use the Guide

Key:

 armed figure

 female

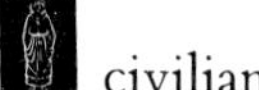 civilian

 child

ecclesiastical

The categories chosen represent the most common figures on brasses. Where these require further explanation, the following abbreviations are used:

Ab, Abbot; ac, Academic; A/B, Archbishop; B, Bishop; F, Flemish; h, heart; j, judge; m, monk; p, palimpsest; s, shroud; SS, saints; symb., symbolic; X, cross

The child symbol stands for an individual brass to a child and does not include the many children who appear with their parents.

Figures are given in chronological order.

Identical dates on the same line but under separate categories, eg

1502 1502

normally indicate two figures on the same brass and, as in the above case, usually husband and wife.

Numbers in parenthesis by a date indicate the total number of figures in that category, eg 1442(2) means that two women are on that brass.

The abbreviation 'P' denotes a *palimpsest* brass, one which has been reused. Over the years many brasses were stolen or defaced, then turned over and another, later figure engraved on them. It is still possible to see both original and newer engraving on such brasses.

North (including the City)

Location					
Acton, St Mary			1558		
Barking,					
St Margaret					1480
					1485
		1493	1493		
		1596	1596		
Bedfont, St Mary		1629			
			1631		
Brentford,					
St Lawrence		1528	1528		
Chelsea, All Saints		1555		1555	
	1625	1625			
CITY					
All Hallows					
Barking, EC3		1437	1437		
		1477	1477		
			1498		
		1518(2)	1518		1510(symb.)
		1533	1533(F)		
	1546	1546			
	1560	1560			
			1591		

Location					
St Andrew Undershaft, EC3		1539	1539	1539	
		1593(2)	1593		
St Bartholomew-the-Less, EC1		1439	1439		
St Dunstan-in-the-West, EC4		1530	1530		
St Helen, Bishopgate, EC2		1465	1465		1482
		1495	1495		1500(ac)
	1510				
	1514				
		1535			
St Martin, Ludgate Hill EC4			1586		
St Olave, Hart St EC3		1516(2)			
		1584	1584		
Temple Church, EC4			1597		
Clerkenwell, St James					1556
Cowley Peachey, W Drayton, St Laurence		1505	1505		
Dagenham, St Peter & St Paul		1479	1479(j)		
Ealing, St Mary		1490	1490		
East Ham, St Mary		1610			
		1622			
Fulham, All Saints		1529(F)			
Greenford, Holy Cross					c1450
		1480			
					c1521
			1544		
Hackney, St John					1521
	1545				
	1562	1562(4)			
					1618
Hadley Green, Barnet, St Mary				1442	
		1500	1500		
		1504	1504		
		1518	1518		
		1614	1614		
Harefield, Northwood St Mary		1444			
		1528	1528 (Sgt/Law)		
	c1535	c1535			
	1537	1537		1537	
		1545	1545		

Location					
Harlington,					
St Peter & St Paul					1419
	1545	1545			
Harrow,					
St Mary	c1370				
	c1390				
					1442
					c1460
					1468(SS)
		1488(3)	1488	1488	
	1579	1579			
		1592	1592		
			1600		
			1603		
Hayes,					
St Mary					1370
	1456				
	1576	1576			
Hendon,					
St Mary				1515	
			1615		
Heston,					
St Leonard		1581			
Hillingdon,					
St John the Baptist	1509	1509			
	1528				
		1579	1579		
Hornchurch,					
St Andrew		1591	1591		
		1602(2)			
		1604	1604		
Hornsey,					
St Mary				c1520	
Ickenham,					
St Giles			c1580		
			1582		
	1584	1584			
Ilford,					
St Mary Chapel			1517		
				1630	
Isleworth,					
All Saints	c1450				
					1561(nun)
			c1590		
				1598	
Islington,					
St Mary	c1535	c1535			
	1546	1546			
Kilburn,					
St Mary					c1450(nun)
Kingsbury,					
St Andrew		1520(2)	1520		

Location					
Leyton					
St Mary		1493			
		c1620	c1620		
Northolt,					
St Mary	1452				
	1560	1560			
					1610
Perivale,					
St Mary		1505(2)	1505		
			c1590		
Pinner,					
St John				1580(P)	
Rainham,					
St Helen & St Giles		c1475			
		c1500	c1500		
Ruislip,					
St Martin		1574	1574		
		1593	1593		
				c1600	
Teddington,					
St Mary		1506	1506		
Tottenham,					
All Hallows		1616	1616		
		1640			
Upminster,					
St Laurence		1455			
			c1530		
		1545	1545(P)		
		c1560			
	1591				
		1626			
Walthamstow,					
St Mary		1543	1543		
			(Mayor)		
		1588	1588(P)		
Wapping,					
Royal Foundation					
of St Katherine	1599	1599			
West Drayton,					
St Martin			c1520		
		1529			
		1581	1581		
Westminster Abbey					1395
					(B, SS)
					1397(A/B)
		1399			
	1438				
	1483				
					1498(Ab)
	1505				
					1561
Westminster					
St Margaret		1597	1597		

Location					
Willesden,					
St Mary		1492	1492		
		1505			
					1517
	1585	1585(2)			
		1609			
South					
Addington,					
St Mary	1540				
		1544	1544		
Barnes,					
St Mary		1508(2)			
Beckenham,					
St George	1552	1552(2)			
		1563			
Beddington,					
St Mary		1414			
		c1430	c1430		
		1432	1432		
	1437				
		1507(2)			
	1520	1520			
Bexley,					
St Mary			1513		
Bromley,					
St Peter & St Paul		1600(2)	1600		
Camberwell,					
St Giles			1497		
			1499		
	1532	1532			
	1538(P)				
		1570	1570		
		1577	1577		
Carshalton,					
All Saints	c1480	c1480			
		1524			1493
Cheam,					
St Dunstan			c1390		
		1458	1458		
			1459		
	c1475				
		1542	1542(P)		
Chelsfield,					
St Mary					1417(S)
					c1420(2)
		c1480			
		1510			
Chislehurst,					
St Nicholas					1482

Location					
Clapham,					
St Peter					c1470
Croydon,					
St John	1562	1562			
Cudham					
Biggin Hill,					
St Peter & St Paul		1503			
Downe,					
Biggin Hill		c1400	c1400		
		c1420	c1420		
		1607	1607		
East Wickham,					
Greenwich,					
St Michael		c1325	c1325		
		1568(3)	1568 (Yeoman)		
Erith,					
St John			1425		
		1435	1435		
		1471			
		1511(2)	1511		
	1537	1537			
Farley,					
Croydon,					
St Mary		1495	1495		
Hayes,					
Bromley,					
St Mary					c1460
					1479
					1523
Lambeth,					
St Mary		1535			
	1545				
Lee, SE12					
St Margaret		1513			
		1582(P)			
	1593				
Mortlake,					
St Mary		1608			
Orpington,					
All Saints					1511
Putney,					
St Mary	1478				
		c1585			
Richmond,					
St Mary Magdalene		1591	1591		
Rotherhithe,					
St Mary		1614	1614		
St Mary Cray					
Orpington		1508(3)	1508		
		1604	1604		
		1747			
			1773		

Location					
Sanderstead, All Saints		1525	1525(P)		
Streatham, St Leonard					1513
Tooting Graveney, St Nicholas		1597	1597		
Wandsworth, All Saints			1420 (Sgt/Law)		
West Wickham, St John					1407 1515

Acknowledgments

Thanks go to the many people who have played a part in this little book's history, from the Reverend Moelwyn Merchant who first introduced me to brasses to the anonymous young man at the cork wholesaler who enabled me to experiment with brasses on cork place mats. It would be impossible to thank individually all the parish priests who have given me permission to rub in their churches, or the many householders who have happily helped me rub coal plates outside their homes. Special thanks for particular aid must go to Mrs Jean Young Farrugia, assistant curator, the National Postal Museum; to Mrs Victoria Moger, Librarian, the Museum of London; to Mrs G. Dodwell of the London Brass Rubbing Centre, and John Page-Phillips of Phillips & Page, for giving details of their organizations and permitting photography at the centres; to Rosemary Harthill for her invaluable help in compiling the Index; to Geoffrey Warren for kindly allowing me to use his illustrations of coal plate rubbings; to Jack Wardle, acting verger at Prestbury parish church for spending so much time pointing out interesting stones and epitaphs there, and to my sister, Kathleen, who gave her rubbings for photography and made forays into Cheshire churchyards on my behalf. Finally, to my husband, Marshall, without whose enthusiastic cooperation as chauffeur, researcher and compiler this book would never have been completed, my heartfelt thanks, as always.

Index

Entries refer to the main text only, not to appendices.
Numbers in italic type refer to illustrations.

David & Charles have a book on it

Vanishing Street Furniture by Geoffrey Warren is the first ever book on a subject which covers the development of public utilities such as street lighting, drinking fountains and pillar boxes from earliest times through the golden nineteenth century age of street furniture. Over 100 illustrations back up the fascinating text in this standard reference work.

Collage by Josephine Lom is intended primarily for beginners of all ages who wish to make collages that do not require much experience, equipment or time. The author explains with simple step-by-step instructions how to make an immensely varied array of collages, some of great beauty, and shows how to let our own imagination work. Illustrated.

Ships in Bottles by Donald Hubbard is a step-by-step guide to a venerable nautical craft. The technique of putting ships in bottles developed during the early years of the nineteenth century. Off-watch seamen whiling away their time used any materials that came to hand – wood, yarn and whalebone to create a most attractive element in nautical folk-art. Early examples are now very scarce and expensive, so for anyone who wants to own one, the easiest way is to make it. In this clearly illustrated study, the author explains which tools, materials and techniques are needed to build a truly beautiful model ship. Here is an authentic maritime craft offering immense satisfaction. Illustrated.

Engraving and Decorating Glass by Barbara Norman. Glass engraving is both an art and a craft, for the artistic and the practical. The various methods of glass decoration are discussed – diamond point, drill and copper wheel engraving, painting, verre eglomise, and mosaics – the author emphasizing the delight of working on pieces that can be used every day in the home or given as presents. The choice of glass and of design for various purposes, and how to set about each of the different techniques, is discussed and illustrated; a summary of the history of glass and how it is made help appreciation of the materials. No special workshop is needed. Illustrated.

Silhouettes: A Living Art by Peggy Hickman. Silhouettes, the beautiful black-and-white sideways portraits produced in quantity in the eighteenth and early nineteenth centuries, are eagerly sought by collectors. This splendidly illustrated background book discussed the artists, their techniques and the revival in profile art with us today. For anyone interested in art forms, in historical portraiture, in cartoons and caricatures, in book illustration or simply in people of the past.

Enjoying Dyes by Hilary Haywood. How to pattern your own fabrics. This book encourages the reader to really enjoy working with dyes. Well illustrated (including gorgeous colour), it simply sets out the main methods of patterning fabrics with dyes, all of which can be done in the home. The author deals with new ideas in fashion, and discusses dyeing projects for children and the use of dyed fabrics for home, offices and public buildings.

The Philatelist's Companion by Bill Gunston. The basic rule in stamp collecting is to know what you are doing. It is possible to make money from collecting stamps, but just as easy to lose it. The author promises that anyone who applies the principles of this book to buying, caring for and generally keeping his collection up-to-date will be able to invest in stamps with at least as much capital appreciation as in a bank and enjoy a fine hobby. Illustrated.

Don't Throw it Away by A. W. Coysh. Here is an entertaining guide to collecting almost every imaginable object from banknotes to valentine cards. Written for the beginner and the amateur enthusiast, A. W. Coysh provides a comprehensively indexed book for easy reference. Illustrated.